TEACHER'S PET PUBLICATIONS

PUZZLE PACK
for
Across Five Aprils
based on the book by
Irene Hunt

Written by
William T. Collins

© 2005 Teacher's Pet Publications
All Rights Reserved

The materials in this packet are copyrighted
by Teacher's Pet Publications, Inc.

These pages may be duplicated by the purchaser
for use in the purchaser's own classroom.

Copying any of these materials and distributing them
for any other purpose is a violation of the copyright laws.

© 2005 Teacher's Pet Publications, Inc.
www.tpet.com

INTRODUCTION
If you already own the LitPlan for this title, this Puzzle Pack will refresh your Unit Resource Materials and Vocabulary Resource Materials sections plus give you additional materials you can substitute into the tests. If you do not already have a complete LitPlan, these pages will give you some supplemental materials to use with your own plan. There are two main groups of materials: one set for unit words (such as characters' names, symbols, places, etc.) and one set for vocabulary words associated with the book.

WORD LIST
There is a word list for both the unit words and the vocabulary words. These lists show you which words are being used in the materials and the clues or definitions being used for those words. You may want to give students a word list with clues/definitions to help them, or you may want students to only have a word list (without clues/definitions) if you want them to work a little harder. Both are available for duplication. The word lists can also be your "calling key" for the bingo games.

FILL IN THE BLANK AND MATCHING
There are 4 each of the fill in the blank and matching worksheets for both the unit and vocabulary words. These pages can be used either as extra worksheets for students or as objective parts of a unit test. They can be done individually if students need extra help or as a whole class activity to review the material covered.

MAGIC SQUARES
The magic squares not only reinforce the material covered but also work on reasoning and math skills. Many teachers have told us that their students really enjoy doing these!

WORD SEARCH PUZZLES
The word search words go in all directions, as indicated on your answer keys. Two of the word search puzzles have the clues listed rather than the words. This makes the puzzle a little more difficult, but it reinforces the material better. Two word search puzzles have words only for students who find the clue puzzles too difficult.

CROSSWORD PUZZLES
Both unit and vocabulary word sections have 4 crossword puzzles.

BINGO CARDS
There are 32 individual bingo cards for the unit words and 32 individual bingo cards for the vocabulary words. You can use your word list as a "call list," calling the words at random and marking them off of your list as you go, or you could use the flash cards by cutting them apart and drawing the words at random from a hat (or box or whatever). To make a better review, you might ask for the definition and spelling of each word as you call it out–or you could call out the definitions and have students tell you the words they need to look for on the puzzle.

JUGGLE LETTERS
The vocabulary juggle letter game is intended to help students learn the spellings of the words. One sheet has the definitions listed on it as an extra help for students who need it or to reinforce the definitions if you choose to do so.

FLASH CARDS
We've included a set of vocabulary flash cards you can duplicate, cut, and fold for your students. Some teachers make a few sets for general use by the class; others make a set for each student. Some teachers duplicate them for each student and have the students cut & fold their own. You can cut out just the words and put them in a hat, have each student pick out one word and write the definition and a sentence for that word. Students then swap words and papers, with the next student adding a sentence of his own under the last one. You can have students swap as many times as you like. Each time the student will read the sentences written prior to his own and then add a sentence. You can cut out the words and definitions separately and play "I Have; Who Has?" Each student in the room draws a word and definition. The first student says, "I have (the name of the word). Who has the definition?" The student with the definition reads it then says, "I have (the name of the vocabulary word she has). Who has the definition?" The round continues until all words and definitions have been given.

Across Five Aprils Unit Word List

No.	Word	Clue/Definition
1.	ADULTS	They were troubled by drought, elections, slavery, secession & talk of war
2.	AMENDMENT	The 13th ____ freed slaves
3.	APPOMATTOX	Courthouse where the South surrendered
4.	BARN	People set the Creighton's on fire
5.	BILL	Went to fight for the South
6.	BLUFF	Ball's ____
7.	BRIDGE	Place where Jethro & Dave Burdow were attacked
8.	BULL	____ Run
9.	CHILDHOOD	Jethro left his behind him in March 1862
10.	CONFEDERATES	Fighters for the South
11.	DAN	Lawrence; Brings news of Tom's death
12.	DANCE	Where Mary had been the night she was killed
13.	DAVE	Burdow who rode with Jethro & saved him
14.	DESERTER	What Eb became by leaving the army
15.	DITCHES	Eb's job was digging these when he rejoined the army
16.	EB	Jethro wrote to Lincoln about his desertion
17.	ELLEN	Jethro's mother
18.	GRANT	Northern general
19.	HENRY	The union began to win after the fall of Fort ____ in Tennessee
20.	JENNY	Married Shad Yale
21.	JETHRO	Young boy who grew up during the Civil War
22.	JOHN	Bill & he were close brothers who had a fight
23.	LEE	Southern general
24.	LINCOLN	President during the Civil War
25.	MANHOOD	Jethro's going to town alone was a step towards his ____.
26.	MARY	Was killed in an accident
27.	MATT	Jethro's father
28.	MILTON	Editor
29.	NANCY	John's wife
30.	PROSPECT	Point ____; deserters' camp
31.	READ	Ellen gave the letter to Jethro because she could not ____.
32.	ROSCOE	Jake; wanted Jethro to bring him a newspaper
33.	SAVANNAH	Sherman's gift to Lincoln
34.	SCARED	Bill told Jethro that being ____ was nothing to be ashamed of
35.	SHADRACH	Teacher
36.	SHILOH	Jethro considered the victory here to be empty like Pittsburgh landing
37.	SUMTER	Confederates fired on this fort and the war started
38.	TOM	Died on the battlefield
39.	TURKEY	Call Eb used in the woods
40.	WASHINGTON	Jenny went there to see Shad
41.	WILSE	Ellen's nephew
42.	WILSON	____'s Creek; battle close to Creighton's home; Union lost
43.	WORTMAN	Mob leader who threatened Jethro

Across Five Aprils Fill In The Blank 1

_____

_____

_____

_____

_____

_____

_____

_____

_____

_____

_____

_____

_____

_____

_____

_____

_____

_____

_____

_____

1. Bill & he were close brothers who had a fight
2. Went to fight for the South
3. Place where Jethro & Dave Burdow were attacked
4. Jethro's father
5. Bill told Jethro that being ____ was nothing to be ashamed of
6. President during the Civil War
7. Jethro's going to town alone was a step towards his ____.
8. Ball's ____
9. Southern general
10. They were troubled by drought, elections, slavery, secession & talk of war
11. Jethro's mother
12. Lawrence; Brings news of Tom's death
13. Sherman's gift to Lincoln
14. Jethro left his behind him in March 1862
15. Jake; wanted Jethro to bring him a newspaper
16. Jenny went there to see Shad
17. Young boy who grew up during the Civil War
18. Editor
19. Teacher
20. Fighters for the South

Across Five Aprils Fill In The Blank 1 Answer Key

JOHN	1. Bill & he were close brothers who had a fight
BILL	2. Went to fight for the South
BRIDGE	3. Place where Jethro & Dave Burdow were attacked
MATT	4. Jethro's father
SCARED	5. Bill told Jethro that being ____ was nothing to be ashamed of
LINCOLN	6. President during the Civil War
MANHOOD	7. Jethro's going to town alone was a step towards his ____.
BLUFF	8. Ball's ____
LEE	9. Southern general
ADULTS	10. They were troubled by drought, elections, slavery, secession & talk of war
ELLEN	11. Jethro's mother
DAN	12. Lawrence; Brings news of Tom's death
SAVANNAH	13. Sherman's gift to Lincoln
CHILDHOOD	14. Jethro left his behind him in March 1862
ROSCOE	15. Jake; wanted Jethro to bring him a newspaper
WASHINGTON	16. Jenny went there to see Shad
JETHRO	17. Young boy who grew up during the Civil War
MILTON	18. Editor
SHADRACH	19. Teacher
CONFEDERATES	20. Fighters for the South

Across Five Aprils Fill In The Blank 2

_____

_____

_____

_____

_____

_____

_____

_____

_____

_____

_____

_____

_____

_____

_____

_____

_____

_____

_____

_____

1. They were troubled by drought, elections, slavery, secession & talk of war
2. Married Shad Yale
3. Jethro considered the victory here to be empty like Pittsburgh landing
4. Jethro's mother
5. Young boy who grew up during the Civil War
6. Eb's job was digging these when he rejoined the army
7. Courthouse where the South surrendered
8. People set the Creighton's on fire
9. The 13th ____ freed slaves
10. John's wife
11. Ball's ____
12. Jethro left his behind him in March 1862
13. Confederates fired on this fort and the war started
14. Fighters for the South
15. ____'s Creek; battle close to Creighton's home; Union lost
16. Place where Jethro & Dave Burdow were attacked
17. Jethro wrote to Lincoln about his desertion
18. Jethro's father
19. Died on the battlefield
20. Southern general

Across Five Aprils Fill In The Blank 2 Answer Key

ADULTS	1. They were troubled by drought, elections, slavery, secession & talk of war
JENNY	2. Married Shad Yale
SHILOH	3. Jethro considered the victory here to be empty like Pittsburgh landing
ELLEN	4. Jethro's mother
JETHRO	5. Young boy who grew up during the Civil War
DITCHES	6. Eb's job was digging these when he rejoined the army
APPOMATTOX	7. Courthouse where the South surrendered
BARN	8. People set the Creighton's on fire
AMENDMENT	9. The 13th ____ freed slaves
NANCY	10. John's wife
BLUFF	11. Ball's ____
CHILDHOOD	12. Jethro left his behind him in March 1862
SUMTER	13. Confederates fired on this fort and the war started
CONFEDERATES	14. Fighters for the South
WILSON	15. ____'s Creek; battle close to Creighton's home; Union lost
BRIDGE	16. Place where Jethro & Dave Burdow were attacked
EB	17. Jethro wrote to Lincoln about his desertion
MATT	18. Jethro's father
TOM	19. Died on the battlefield
LEE	20. Southern general

Across Five Aprils Fill In The Blank 3

_____

_____

_____

_____

_____

_____

_____

_____

_____

_____

_____

_____

_____

_____

_____

_____

_____

_____

_____

_____

1. Editor

2. Point ____; deserters' camp

3. Southern general

4. They were troubled by drought, elections, slavery, secession & talk of war

5. Ellen gave the letter to Jethro because she could not ____.

6. The 13th ____ freed slaves

7. Northern general

8. People set the Creighton's on fire

9. Jethro's father

10. ____ Run

11. Call Eb used in the woods

12. What Eb became by leaving the army

13. Went to fight for the South

14. Sherman's gift to Lincoln

15. Bill & he were close brothers who had a fight

16. Burdow who rode with Jethro & saved him

17. The union began to win after the fall of Fort ____ in Tennessee

18. Jethro left his behind him in March 1862

19. Jake; wanted Jethro to bring him a newspaper

20. Jethro considered the victory here to be empty like Pittsburgh landing

Across Five Aprils Fill In The Blank 3 Answer Key

MILTON	1. Editor
PROSPECT	2. Point ____; deserters' camp
LEE	3. Southern general
ADULTS	4. They were troubled by drought, elections, slavery, secession & talk of war
READ	5. Ellen gave the letter to Jethro because she could not ____.
AMENDMENT	6. The 13th ____ freed slaves
GRANT	7. Northern general
BARN	8. People set the Creighton's on fire
MATT	9. Jethro's father
BULL	10. ____ Run
TURKEY	11. Call Eb used in the woods
DESERTER	12. What Eb became by leaving the army
BILL	13. Went to fight for the South
SAVANNAH	14. Sherman's gift to Lincoln
JOHN	15. Bill & he were close brothers who had a fight
DAVE	16. Burdow who rode with Jethro & saved him
HENRY	17. The union began to win after the fall of Fort ____ in Tennessee
CHILDHOOD	18. Jethro left his behind him in March 1862
ROSCOE	19. Jake; wanted Jethro to bring him a newspaper
SHILOH	20. Jethro considered the victory here to be empty like Pittsburgh landing

Across Five Aprils Fill In The Blank 4

_____

_____

_____

_____

_____

_____

_____

_____

_____

_____

_____

_____

_____

_____

_____

_____

_____

_____

_____

_____

1. Jake; wanted Jethro to bring him a newspaper
2. Jethro wrote to Lincoln about his desertion
3. Fighters for the South
4. Point ____; deserters' camp
5. Died on the battlefield
6. Call Eb used in the woods
7. Teacher
8. Married Shad Yale
9. Sherman's gift to Lincoln
10. Where Mary had been the night she was killed
11. Jenny went there to see Shad
12. Went to fight for the South
13. Bill told Jethro that being ____ was nothing to be ashamed of
14. People set the Creighton's on fire
15. Courthouse where the South surrendered
16. John's wife
17. Northern general
18. Jethro considered the victory here to be empty like Pittsburgh landing
19. ____ Run
20. Bill & he were close brothers who had a fight

Across Five Aprils Fill In The Blank 4 Answer Key

ROSCOE	1. Jake; wanted Jethro to bring him a newspaper
EB	2. Jethro wrote to Lincoln about his desertion
CONFEDERATES	3. Fighters for the South
PROSPECT	4. Point ____; deserters' camp
TOM	5. Died on the battlefield
TURKEY	6. Call Eb used in the woods
SHADRACH	7. Teacher
JENNY	8. Married Shad Yale
SAVANNAH	9. Sherman's gift to Lincoln
DANCE	10. Where Mary had been the night she was killed
WASHINGTON	11. Jenny went there to see Shad
BILL	12. Went to fight for the South
SCARED	13. Bill told Jethro that being ____ was nothing to be ashamed of
BARN	14. People set the Creighton's on fire
APPOMATTOX	15. Courthouse where the South surrendered
NANCY	16. John's wife
GRANT	17. Northern general
SHILOH	18. Jethro considered the victory here to be empty like Pittsburgh landing
BULL	19. ____ Run
JOHN	20. Bill & he were close brothers who had a fight

Across Five Aprils Matching 1

___ 1. JENNY A. ____ Run
___ 2. JETHRO B. Jake; wanted Jethro to bring him a newspaper
___ 3. DAN C. Ellen gave the letter to Jethro because she could not ____.
___ 4. SHILOH D. Editor
___ 5. JOHN E. Jethro considered the victory here to be empty like Pittsburgh landing
___ 6. READ F. Courthouse where the South surrendered
___ 7. TOM G. People set the Creighton's on fire
___ 8. EB H. Jethro left his behind him in March 1862
___ 9. AMENDMENT I. John's wife
___10. ADULTS J. Mob leader who threatened Jethro
___11. WORTMAN K. Young boy who grew up during the Civil War
___12. SAVANNAH L. Married Shad Yale
___13. SUMTER M. Bill & he were close brothers who had a fight
___14. NANCY N. Jenny went there to see Shad
___15. APPOMATTOX O. Confederates fired on this fort and the war started
___16. BULL P. Fighters for the South
___17. DESERTER Q. Jethro wrote to Lincoln about his desertion
___18. WASHINGTON R. The 13th ____ freed slaves
___19. MILTON S. Northern general
___20. BARN T. Was killed in an accident
___21. CHILDHOOD U. They were troubled by drought, elections, slavery, secession & talk of war
___22. CONFEDERATES V. Died on the battlefield
___23. ROSCOE W. Sherman's gift to Lincoln
___24. GRANT X. Lawrence; Brings news of Tom's death
___25. MARY Y. What Eb became by leaving the army

Across Five Aprils Matching 1 Answer Key

L - 1.	JENNY	A.	____ Run
K - 2.	JETHRO	B.	Jake; wanted Jethro to bring him a newspaper
X - 3.	DAN	C.	Ellen gave the letter to Jethro because she could not ____.
E - 4.	SHILOH	D.	Editor
M - 5.	JOHN	E.	Jethro considered the victory here to be empty like Pittsburgh landing
C - 6.	READ	F.	Courthouse where the South surrendered
V - 7.	TOM	G.	People set the Creighton's on fire
Q - 8.	EB	H.	Jethro left his behind him in March 1862
R - 9.	AMENDMENT	I.	John's wife
U -10.	ADULTS	J.	Mob leader who threatened Jethro
J -11.	WORTMAN	K.	Young boy who grew up during the Civil War
W -12.	SAVANNAH	L.	Married Shad Yale
O -13.	SUMTER	M.	Bill & he were close brothers who had a fight
I -14.	NANCY	N.	Jenny went there to see Shad
F -15.	APPOMATTOX	O.	Confederates fired on this fort and the war started
A -16.	BULL	P.	Fighters for the South
Y -17.	DESERTER	Q.	Jethro wrote to Lincoln about his desertion
N -18.	WASHINGTON	R.	The 13th ____ freed slaves
D -19.	MILTON	S.	Northern general
G -20.	BARN	T.	Was killed in an accident
H -21.	CHILDHOOD	U.	They were troubled by drought, elections, slavery, secession & talk of war
P -22.	CONFEDERATES	V.	Died on the battlefield
B -23.	ROSCOE	W.	Sherman's gift to Lincoln
S -24.	GRANT	X.	Lawrence; Brings news of Tom's death
T -25.	MARY	Y.	What Eb became by leaving the army

Across Five Aprils Matching 2

___ 1. MATT
___ 2. SAVANNAH
___ 3. SCARED
___ 4. BILL
___ 5. BRIDGE
___ 6. TURKEY
___ 7. ADULTS
___ 8. GRANT
___ 9. HENRY
___10. ROSCOE
___11. CONFEDERATES
___12. APPOMATTOX
___13. BLUFF
___14. AMENDMENT
___15. WORTMAN
___16. READ
___17. EB
___18. MANHOOD
___19. LEE
___20. SHADRACH
___21. DESERTER
___22. DAN
___23. WILSON
___24. WILSE
___25. SHILOH

A. Jethro's father
B. Lawrence; Brings news of Tom's death
C. They were troubled by drought, elections, slavery, secession & talk of war
D. Southern general
E. Went to fight for the South
F. Place where Jethro & Dave Burdow were attacked
G. Jake; wanted Jethro to bring him a newspaper
H. Fighters for the South
I. Teacher
J. Sherman's gift to Lincoln
K. ____'s Creek; battle close to Creighton's home; Union lost
L. The union began to win after the fall of Fort ____ in Tennessee
M. Bill told Jethro that being ____ was nothing to be ashamed of
N. The 13th ____ freed slaves
O. Ellen gave the letter to Jethro because she could not ____.
P. Mob leader who threatened Jethro
Q. Ellen's nephew
R. Ball's ____
S. Call Eb used in the woods
T. Jethro's going to town alone was a step towards his ____.
U. Northern general
V. Jethro wrote to Lincoln about his desertion
W. Courthouse where the South surrendered
X. What Eb became by leaving the army
Y. Jethro considered the victory here to be empty like Pittsburgh landing

Across Five Aprils Matching 2 Answer Key

A - 1. MATT	A.	Jethro's father
J - 2. SAVANNAH	B.	Lawrence; Brings news of Tom's death
M - 3. SCARED	C.	They were troubled by drought, elections, slavery, secession & talk of war
E - 4. BILL	D.	Southern general
F - 5. BRIDGE	E.	Went to fight for the South
S - 6. TURKEY	F.	Place where Jethro & Dave Burdow were attacked
C - 7. ADULTS	G.	Jake; wanted Jethro to bring him a newspaper
U - 8. GRANT	H.	Fighters for the South
L - 9. HENRY	I.	Teacher
G -10. ROSCOE	J.	Sherman's gift to Lincoln
H -11. CONFEDERATES	K.	____'s Creek; battle close to Creighton's home; Union lost
W -12. APPOMATTOX	L.	The union began to win after the fall of Fort ____ in Tennessee
R -13. BLUFF	M.	Bill told Jethro that being ____ was nothing to be ashamed of
N -14. AMENDMENT	N.	The 13th ____ freed slaves
P -15. WORTMAN	O.	Ellen gave the letter to Jethro because she could not ____.
O -16. READ	P.	Mob leader who threatened Jethro
V -17. EB	Q.	Ellen's nephew
T -18. MANHOOD	R.	Ball's ____
D -19. LEE	S.	Call Eb used in the woods
I - 20. SHADRACH	T.	Jethro's going to town alone was a step towards his ____.
X -21. DESERTER	U.	Northern general
B -22. DAN	V.	Jethro wrote to Lincoln about his desertion
K -23. WILSON	W.	Courthouse where the South surrendered
Q -24. WILSE	X.	What Eb became by leaving the army
Y -25. SHILOH	Y.	Jethro considered the victory here to be empty like Pittsburgh landing

Across Five Aprils Matching 3

___ 1. JETHRO A. Where Mary had been the night she was killed

___ 2. BARN B. Bill & he were close brothers who had a fight

___ 3. LINCOLN C. People set the Creighton's on fire

___ 4. ADULTS D. Northern general

___ 5. SHILOH E. Young boy who grew up during the Civil War

___ 6. ELLEN F. Confederates fired on this fort and the war started

___ 7. DANCE G. Sherman's gift to Lincoln

___ 8. CONFEDERATES H. The union began to win after the fall of Fort ____ in Tennessee

___ 9. APPOMATTOX I. Teacher

___ 10. AMENDMENT J. Jenny went there to see Shad

___ 11. BILL K. Jethro's mother

___ 12. SUMTER L. John's wife

___ 13. NANCY M. Place where Jethro & Dave Burdow were attacked

___ 14. WASHINGTON N. Went to fight for the South

___ 15. DAN O. Fighters for the South

___ 16. HENRY P. The 13th ____ freed slaves

___ 17. PROSPECT Q. They were troubled by drought, elections, slavery, secession & talk of war

___ 18. BRIDGE R. President during the Civil War

___ 19. GRANT S. Jethro considered the victory here to be empty like Pittsburgh landing

___ 20. MANHOOD T. Jethro left his behind him in March 1862

___ 21. SAVANNAH U. Courthouse where the South surrendered

___ 22. LEE V. Jethro's going to town alone was a step towards his ____.

___ 23. CHILDHOOD W. Point ____; deserters' camp

___ 24. SHADRACH X. Lawrence; Brings news of Tom's death

___ 25. JOHN Y. Southern general

Across Five Aprils Matching 3 Answer Key

E - 1. JETHRO	A.	Where Mary had been the night she was killed
C - 2. BARN	B.	Bill & he were close brothers who had a fight
R - 3. LINCOLN	C.	People set the Creighton's on fire
Q - 4. ADULTS	D.	Northern general
S - 5. SHILOH	E.	Young boy who grew up during the Civil War
K - 6. ELLEN	F.	Confederates fired on this fort and the war started
A - 7. DANCE	G.	Sherman's gift to Lincoln
O - 8. CONFEDERATES	H.	The union began to win after the fall of Fort ____ in Tennessee
U - 9. APPOMATTOX	I.	Teacher
P - 10. AMENDMENT	J.	Jenny went there to see Shad
N - 11. BILL	K.	Jethro's mother
F - 12. SUMTER	L.	John's wife
L - 13. NANCY	M.	Place where Jethro & Dave Burdow were attacked
J - 14. WASHINGTON	N.	Went to fight for the South
X - 15. DAN	O.	Fighters for the South
H - 16. HENRY	P.	The 13th ____ freed slaves
W - 17. PROSPECT	Q.	They were troubled by drought, elections, slavery, secession & talk of war
M - 18. BRIDGE	R.	President during the Civil War
D - 19. GRANT	S.	Jethro considered the victory here to be empty like Pittsburgh landing
V - 20. MANHOOD	T.	Jethro left his behind him in March 1862
G - 21. SAVANNAH	U.	Courthouse where the South surrendered
Y - 22. LEE	V.	Jethro's going to town alone was a step towards his ____.
T - 23. CHILDHOOD	W.	Point ____; deserters' camp
I - 24. SHADRACH	X.	Lawrence; Brings news of Tom's death
B - 25. JOHN	Y.	Southern general

Across Five Aprils Matching 4

___ 1. JENNY
___ 2. LEE
___ 3. WORTMAN
___ 4. EB
___ 5. BARN
___ 6. BLUFF
___ 7. WASHINGTON
___ 8. DESERTER
___ 9. DAVE
___ 10. HENRY
___ 11. APPOMATTOX
___ 12. READ
___ 13. BILL
___ 14. ROSCOE
___ 15. TURKEY
___ 16. SHILOH
___ 17. JETHRO
___ 18. CONFEDERATES
___ 19. ELLEN
___ 20. MILTON
___ 21. ADULTS
___ 22. WILSE
___ 23. SUMTER
___ 24. WILSON
___ 25. PROSPECT

A. Married Shad Yale
B. Courthouse where the South surrendered
C. Jethro wrote to Lincoln about his desertion
D. ____'s Creek; battle close to Creighton's home; Union lost
E. Southern general
F. The union began to win after the fall of Fort ____ in Tennessee
G. Fighters for the South
H. Jake; wanted Jethro to bring him a newspaper
I. Call Eb used in the woods
J. Burdow who rode with Jethro & saved him
K. Went to fight for the South
L. People set the Creighton's on fire
M. Editor
N. Young boy who grew up during the Civil War
O. Jethro's mother
P. What Eb became by leaving the army
Q. Ball's ____
R. They were troubled by drought, elections, slavery, secession & talk of war
S. Point ____; deserters' camp
T. Jenny went there to see Shad
U. Jethro considered the victory here to be empty like Pittsburgh landing
V. Ellen's nephew
W. Confederates fired on this fort and the war started
X. Mob leader who threatened Jethro
Y. Ellen gave the letter to Jethro because she could not ____.

Across Five Aprils Matching 4 Answer Key

A - 1. JENNY	A.	Married Shad Yale
E - 2. LEE	B.	Courthouse where the South surrendered
X - 3. WORTMAN	C.	Jethro wrote to Lincoln about his desertion
C - 4. EB	D.	____'s Creek; battle close to Creighton's home; Union lost
L - 5. BARN	E.	Southern general
Q - 6. BLUFF	F.	The union began to win after the fall of Fort ____ in Tennessee
T - 7. WASHINGTON	G.	Fighters for the South
P - 8. DESERTER	H.	Jake; wanted Jethro to bring him a newspaper
J - 9. DAVE	I.	Call Eb used in the woods
F - 10. HENRY	J.	Burdow who rode with Jethro & saved him
B - 11. APPOMATTOX	K.	Went to fight for the South
Y - 12. READ	L.	People set the Creighton's on fire
K - 13. BILL	M.	Editor
H - 14. ROSCOE	N.	Young boy who grew up during the Civil War
I - 15. TURKEY	O.	Jethro's mother
U - 16. SHILOH	P.	What Eb became by leaving the army
N - 17. JETHRO	Q.	Ball's ____
G - 18. CONFEDERATES	R.	They were troubled by drought, elections, slavery, secession & talk of war
O - 19. ELLEN	S.	Point ____; deserters' camp
M - 20. MILTON	T.	Jenny went there to see Shad
R - 21. ADULTS	U.	Jethro considered the victory here to be empty like Pittsburgh landing
V - 22. WILSE	V.	Ellen's nephew
W - 23. SUMTER	W.	Confederates fired on this fort and the war started
D - 24. WILSON	X.	Mob leader who threatened Jethro
S - 25. PROSPECT	Y.	Ellen gave the letter to Jethro because she could not ____.

Across Five Aprils Magic Squares 1

Match the definition with the vocabulary word. Put your answers in the magic squares below. When your answers are correct, all columns and rows will add to the same number.

A. WASHINGTON
B. BLUFF
C. BILL
D. PROSPECT
E. APPOMATTOX
F. MANHOOD
G. CHILDHOOD
H. TURKEY
I. DESERTER
J. ADULTS
K. ELLEN
L. CONFEDERATES
M. ROSCOE
N. DANCE
O. NANCY
P. MARY

1. Ball's ____
2. Jethro left his behind him in March 1862
3. Jethro's mother
4. Where Mary had been the night she was killed
5. Jake; wanted Jethro to bring him a newspaper
6. Fighters for the South
7. Call Eb used in the woods
8. Jenny went there to see Shad
9. Was killed in an accident
10. What Eb became by leaving the army
11. Courthouse where the South surrendered
12. Point ____; deserters' camp
13. Went to fight for the South
14. Jethro's going to town alone was a step towards his ____.
15. They were troubled by drought, elections, slavery, secession & talk of war
16. John's wife

A=	B=	C=	D=
E=	F=	G=	H=
I=	J=	K=	L=
M=	N=	O=	P=

Across Five Aprils Magic Squares 1 Answer Key

Match the definition with the vocabulary word. Put your answers in the magic squares below. When your answers are correct, all columns and rows will add to the same number.

A. WASHINGTON
B. BLUFF
C. BILL
D. PROSPECT
E. APPOMATTOX
F. MANHOOD
G. CHILDHOOD
H. TURKEY
I. DESERTER
J. ADULTS
K. ELLEN
L. CONFEDERATES
M. ROSCOE
N. DANCE
O. NANCY
P. MARY

1. Ball's ____
2. Jethro left his behind him in March 1862
3. Jethro's mother
4. Where Mary had been the night she was killed
5. Jake; wanted Jethro to bring him a newspaper
6. Fighters for the South
7. Call Eb used in the woods
8. Jenny went there to see Shad
9. Was killed in an accident
10. What Eb became by leaving the army
11. Courthouse where the South surrendered
12. Point ____; deserters' camp
13. Went to fight for the South
14. Jethro's going to town alone was a step towards his ____.
15. They were troubled by drought, elections, slavery, secession & talk of war
16. John's wife

A=8	B=1	C=13	D=12
E=11	F=14	G=2	H=7
I=10	J=15	K=3	L=6
M=5	N=4	O=16	P=9

Across Five Aprils Magic Squares 2

Match the definition with the vocabulary word. Put your answers in the magic squares below. When your answers are correct, all columns and rows will add to the same number.

A. TOM
B. WILSE
C. WORTMAN
D. CHILDHOOD
E. TURKEY
F. NANCY
G. BILL
H. SHADRACH
I. WILSON
J. HENRY
K. BRIDGE
L. LEE
M. MANHOOD
N. DANCE
O. DESERTER
P. BULL

1. Where Mary had been the night she was killed
2. Went to fight for the South
3. Southern general
4. Died on the battlefield
5. Place where Jethro & Dave Burdow were attacked
6. Ellen's nephew
7. Jethro's going to town alone was a step towards his ____.
8. Teacher
9. Call Eb used in the woods
10. ____ Run
11. Mob leader who threatened Jethro
12. The union began to win after the fall of Fort ____ in Tennessee
13. Jethro left his behind him in March 1862
14. ____'s Creek; battle close to Creighton's home; Union lost
15. John's wife
16. What Eb became by leaving the army

A=	B=	C=	D=
E=	F=	G=	H=
I=	J=	K=	L=
M=	N=	O=	P=

Across Five Aprils Magic Squares 2 Answer Key

Match the definition with the vocabulary word. Put your answers in the magic squares below. When your answers are correct, all columns and rows will add to the same number.

A. TOM
B. WILSE
C. WORTMAN
D. CHILDHOOD
E. TURKEY
F. NANCY
G. BILL
H. SHADRACH
I. WILSON
J. HENRY
K. BRIDGE
L. LEE
M. MANHOOD
N. DANCE
O. DESERTER
P. BULL

1. Where Mary had been the night she was killed
2. Went to fight for the South
3. Southern general
4. Died on the battlefield
5. Place where Jethro & Dave Burdow were attacked
6. Ellen's nephew
7. Jethro's going to town alone was a step towards his ____.
8. Teacher
9. Call Eb used in the woods
10. ____ Run
11. Mob leader who threatened Jethro
12. The union began to win after the fall of Fort ____ in Tennessee
13. Jethro left his behind him in March 1862
14. ____'s Creek; battle close to Creighton's home; Union lost
15. John's wife
16. What Eb became by leaving the army

A=4	B=6	C=11	D=13
E=9	F=15	G=2	H=8
I=14	J=12	K=5	L=3
M=7	N=1	O=16	P=10

Across Five Aprils Magic Squares 3

Match the definition with the vocabulary word. Put your answers in the magic squares below. When your answers are correct, all columns and rows will add to the same number.

A. MARY
B. ADULTS
C. MILTON
D. MANHOOD
E. SAVANNAH
F. BRIDGE
G. DITCHES
H. DESERTER
I. BULL
J. GRANT
K. READ
L. CHILDHOOD
M. SHILOH
N. NANCY
O. WORTMAN
P. BLUFF

1. Mob leader who threatened Jethro
2. Jethro's going to town alone was a step towards his ____.
3. Northern general
4. Sherman's gift to Lincoln
5. ____ Run
6. Place where Jethro & Dave Burdow were attacked
7. Ball's ____
8. Editor
9. What Eb became by leaving the army
10. Ellen gave the letter to Jethro because she could not ____.
11. Was killed in an accident
12. John's wife
13. They were troubled by drought, elections, slavery, secession & talk of war
14. Jethro considered the victory here to be empty like Pittsburgh landing
15. Eb's job was digging these when he rejoined the army
16. Jethro left his behind him in March 1862

A=	B=	C=	D=
E=	F=	G=	H=
I=	J=	K=	L=
M=	N=	O=	P=

Across Five Aprils Magic Squares 3 Answer Key

Match the definition with the vocabulary word. Put your answers in the magic squares below. When your answers are correct, all columns and rows will add to the same number.

A. MARY
B. ADULTS
C. MILTON
D. MANHOOD
E. SAVANNAH
F. BRIDGE
G. DITCHES
H. DESERTER
I. BULL
J. GRANT
K. READ
L. CHILDHOOD
M. SHILOH
N. NANCY
O. WORTMAN
P. BLUFF

1. Mob leader who threatened Jethro
2. Jethro's going to town alone was a step towards his ____.
3. Northern general
4. Sherman's gift to Lincoln
5. ____ Run
6. Place where Jethro & Dave Burdow were attacked
7. Ball's ____
8. Editor
9. What Eb became by leaving the army
10. Ellen gave the letter to Jethro because she could not ____.
11. Was killed in an accident
12. John's wife
13. They were troubled by drought, elections, slavery, secession & talk of war
14. Jethro considered the victory here to be empty like Pittsburgh landing
15. Eb's job was digging these when he rejoined the army
16. Jethro left his behind him in March 1862

A=11	B=13	C=8	D=2
E=4	F=6	G=15	H=9
I=5	J=3	K=10	L=16
M=14	N=12	O=1	P=7

Across Five Aprils Magic Squares 4

Match the definition with the vocabulary word. Put your answers in the magic squares below. When your answers are correct, all columns and rows will add to the same number.

A. SHILOH
B. CHILDHOOD
C. BILL
D. MATT
E. TOM
F. NANCY
G. WASHINGTON
H. DITCHES
I. BARN
J. ELLEN
K. MANHOOD
L. MILTON
M. DESERTER
N. ADULTS
O. SUMTER
P. ROSCOE

1. John's wife
2. People set the Creighton's on fire
3. Confederates fired on this fort and the war started
4. Jethro's father
5. What Eb became by leaving the army
6. Jethro left his behind him in March 1862
7. Eb's job was digging these when he rejoined the army
8. Jethro's going to town alone was a step towards his _____.
9. Went to fight for the South
10. Jake; wanted Jethro to bring him a newspaper
11. Jethro's mother
12. Died on the battlefield
13. Editor
14. Jenny went there to see Shad
15. Jethro considered the victory here to be empty like Pittsburgh landing
16. They were troubled by drought, elections, slavery, secession & talk of war war

A=	B=	C=	D=
E=	F=	G=	H=
I=	J=	K=	L=
M=	N=	O=	P=

Across Five Aprils Magic Squares 4 Answer Key

Match the definition with the vocabulary word. Put your answers in the magic squares below. When your answers are correct, all columns and rows will add to the same number.

A. SHILOH
B. CHILDHOOD
C. BILL
D. MATT
E. TOM
F. NANCY
G. WASHINGTON
H. DITCHES
I. BARN
J. ELLEN
K. MANHOOD
L. MILTON
M. DESERTER
N. ADULTS
O. SUMTER
P. ROSCOE

1. John's wife
2. People set the Creighton's on fire
3. Confederates fired on this fort and the war started
4. Jethro's father
5. What Eb became by leaving the army
6. Jethro left his behind him in March 1862
7. Eb's job was digging these when he rejoined the army
8. Jethro's going to town alone was a step towards his _____.
9. Went to fight for the South
10. Jake; wanted Jethro to bring him a newspaper
11. Jethro's mother
12. Died on the battlefield
13. Editor
14. Jenny went there to see Shad
15. Jethro considered the victory here to be empty like Pittsburgh landing
16. They were troubled by drought, elections, slavery, secession & talk of war war

A=15	B=6	C=9	D=4
E=12	F=1	G=14	H=7
I=2	J=11	K=8	L=13
M=5	N=16	O=3	P=10

Across Five Aprils Word Search 1

```
T Z N D Q X Y T B M R Q X E S T O E W Y
U M R L E W N B C A S E S V H S R O I N
R H C L G S N B E R H L A A F P H C L Z
K B R I D G E S B Y I N A D U L T S S Y
E M P B C E J R R W L J O I S G E O O S
Y I R T L T S N T J O O Z T T C J R N G
Y L O T C J E A H E H C W C O L A W G X
M T S Z O H H D V N R N O H M R N R K T
N O P V N F T M A A H V R E H R F E E T
M N E F F N X M N O N Z T S A P K T A D
E A C K E W R J J D V N M B G P T M P Q
L M T S D B U L L A Y N A N C Y F U P Y
L H G T E X Q F I N M F N H C F M S O Y
E C J R R K D Z N C G E W Q U W B R M T
N A G F A D R S C E W F N L C P K J A P
H R C N T N M W O K D L B D H C C C T C
D D K V E T T N L K V F K M M V K T T P
S A W B S R G Y N T W K P F Z E G B O X
C H I L D H O O D H K W J F C H N Q X F
X S Z V W A S H I N G T O N R L J T W C
```

Call Eb used in the woods (6)
Ball's ____ (5)
Bill & he were close brothers who had a fight (4)
Bill told Jethro that being ____ was nothing to be ashamed of (6)
Burdow who rode with Jethro & saved him (4)
Confederates fired on this fort and the war started (6)
Courthouse where the South surrendered (10)
Died on the battlefield (3)
Eb's job was digging these when he rejoined the army (7)
Editor (6)
Ellen gave the letter to Jethro because she could not ____. (4)
Ellen's nephew (5)
Fighters for the South (12)
Jake; wanted Jethro to bring him a newspaper (6)
Jenny went there to see Shad (10)
Jethro considered the victory here to be empty like Pittsburgh landing (6)
Jethro left his behind him in March 1862 (9)
Jethro wrote to Lincoln about his desertion (2)
Jethro's father (4)
Jethro's going to town alone was a step towards his ____. (7)
Jethro's mother (5)
John's wife (5)
Lawrence; Brings news of Tom's death (3)
Married Shad Yale (5)
Mob leader who threatened Jethro (7)
Northern general (5)

People set the Creighton's on fire (4)
Place where Jethro & Dave Burdow were attacked (6)
Point ____; deserters' camp (8)
President during the Civil War (7)
Sherman's gift to Lincoln (8)
Southern general (3)
Teacher (8)
The 13th ____ freed slaves (9)
The union began to win after the fall of Fort ____ in Tennessee (5)
They were troubled by drought, elections, slavery, secession & talk of war (6)
Was killed in an accident (4)
Went to fight for the South (4)
What Eb became by leaving the army (8)
Where Mary had been the night she was killed (5)
Young boy who grew up during the Civil War (6)
____ Run (4)
____'s Creek; battle close to Creighton's home; Union lost (6)

Across Five Aprils Word Search 1 Answer Key

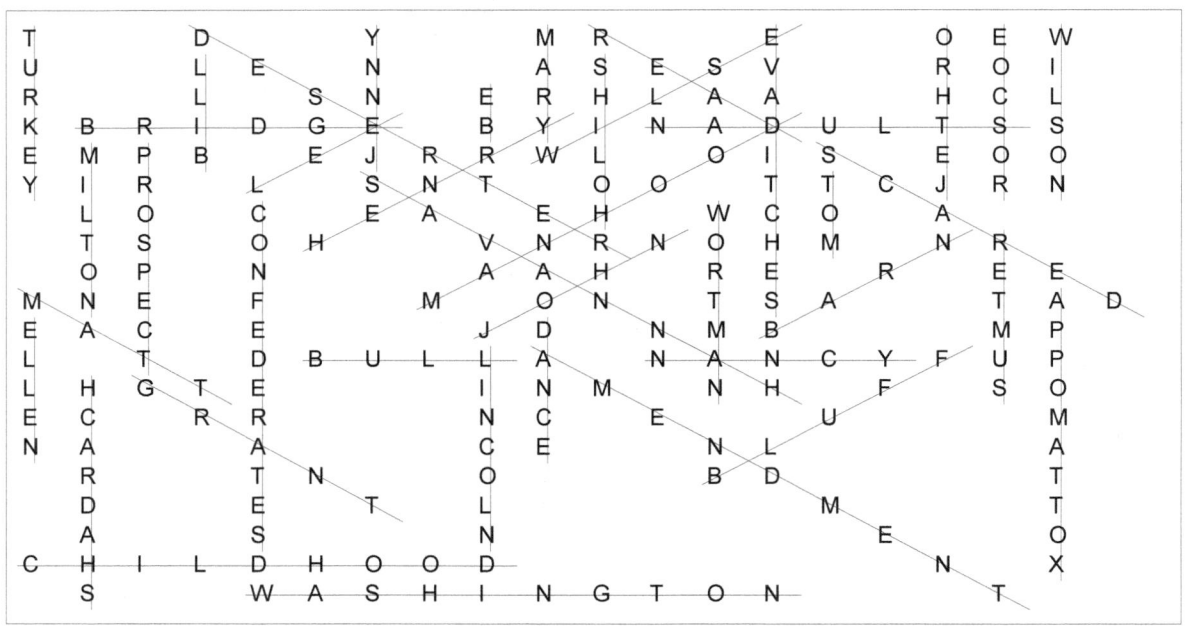

Call Eb used in the woods (6)
Ball's ____ (5)
Bill & he were close brothers who had a fight (4)
Bill told Jethro that being ____ was nothing to be ashamed of (6)
Burdow who rode with Jethro & saved him (4)
Confederates fired on this fort and the war started (6)
Courthouse where the South surrendered (10)
Died on the battlefield (3)
Eb's job was digging these when he rejoined the army (7)
Editor (6)
Ellen gave the letter to Jethro because she could not ____. (4)
Ellen's nephew (5)
Fighters for the South (12)
Jake; wanted Jethro to bring him a newspaper (6)
Jenny went there to see Shad (10)
Jethro considered the victory here to be empty like Pittsburgh landing (6)
Jethro left his behind him in March 1862 (9)
Jethro wrote to Lincoln about his desertion (2)
Jethro's father (4)
Jethro's going to town alone was a step towards his ____. (7)
Jethro's mother (5)
John's wife (5)
Lawrence; Brings news of Tom's death (3)
Married Shad Yale (5)
Mob leader who threatened Jethro (7)
Northern general (5)

People set the Creighton's on fire (4)
Place where Jethro & Dave Burdow were attacked (6)
Point ____; deserters' camp (8)
President during the Civil War (7)
Sherman's gift to Lincoln (8)
Southern general (3)
Teacher (8)
The 13th ____ freed slaves (9)
The union began to win after the fall of Fort ____ in Tennessee (5)
They were troubled by drought, elections, slavery, secession & talk of war (6)
Was killed in an accident (4)
Went to fight for the South (4)
What Eb became by leaving the army (8)
Where Mary had been the night she was killed (5)
Young boy who grew up during the Civil War (6)
____ Run (4)
____'s Creek; battle close to Creighton's home; Union lost (6)

Across Five Aprils Word Search 2

```
V X H D S V D P R B P W X M M Z Y G P C
T P T I R U D L R X R C M N L N X H Q K
N J W T H J M D A B O I V J N V T J Y P
E K O C X V M T A P S D D E B A D R R D
M A N H O O D B E N P O J G R A N T A Y
D D E E N T L V O R E O T W E E O C M T
N U L S R U A T C V C H M R H M T B Y Y
E L L M F D G S S J T D W A E S L I W D
M T E F A N N S O F E L W E T W I X Y W
A S Z L I T S R R S S I L I J T M W H J
G G V H M H T R E P H H B W L R O N L J
K P S T H M X R M F A C T L K S R X G H
Q A F F V H T L Q S D B I Q D A O V N C
W S C A R E D O W L R B Z V B N D N K C
T O S P R Q R V S D A Y K U Q C A F W L
G L R T S H N Z P T C G L J G J N T H R
V F H T T B P C V H H L P C R B C N S D
W H Q E M S H I L O H P T U R K E Y F M
K F J T S A V A N N A H Q X G P R V W Z
L I N C O L N C O N F E D E R A T E S T
```

Call Eb used in the woods (6)
Ball's ____ (5)
Bill & he were close brothers who had a fight (4)
Bill told Jethro that being ____ was nothing to be ashamed of (6)
Burdow who rode with Jethro & saved him (4)
Confederates fired on this fort and the war started (6)
Courthouse where the South surrendered (10)
Died on the battlefield (3)
Eb's job was digging these when he rejoined the army (7)
Editor (6)
Ellen gave the letter to Jethro because she could not ____. (4)
Ellen's nephew (5)
Fighters for the South (12)
Jake; wanted Jethro to bring him a newspaper (6)
Jenny went there to see Shad (10)
Jethro considered the victory here to be empty like Pittsburgh landing (6)
Jethro left his behind him in March 1862 (9)
Jethro wrote to Lincoln about his desertion (2)
Jethro's father (4)
Jethro's going to town alone was a step towards his ____. (7)
Jethro's mother (5)
John's wife (5)
Lawrence; Brings news of Tom's death (3)
Married Shad Yale (5)
Mob leader who threatened Jethro (7)
Northern general (5)

People set the Creighton's on fire (4)
Place where Jethro & Dave Burdow were attacked (6)
Point ____; deserters' camp (8)
President during the Civil War (7)
Sherman's gift to Lincoln (8)
Southern general (3)
Teacher (8)
The 13th ____ freed slaves (9)
The union began to win after the fall of Fort ____ in Tennessee (5)
They were troubled by drought, elections, slavery, secession & talk of war (6)
Was killed in an accident (4)
Went to fight for the South (4)
What Eb became by leaving the army (8)
Where Mary had been the night she was killed (5)
Young boy who grew up during the Civil War (6)
____ Run (4)
____'s Creek; battle close to Creighton's home; Union lost (6)

Across Five Aprils Word Search 2 Answer Key

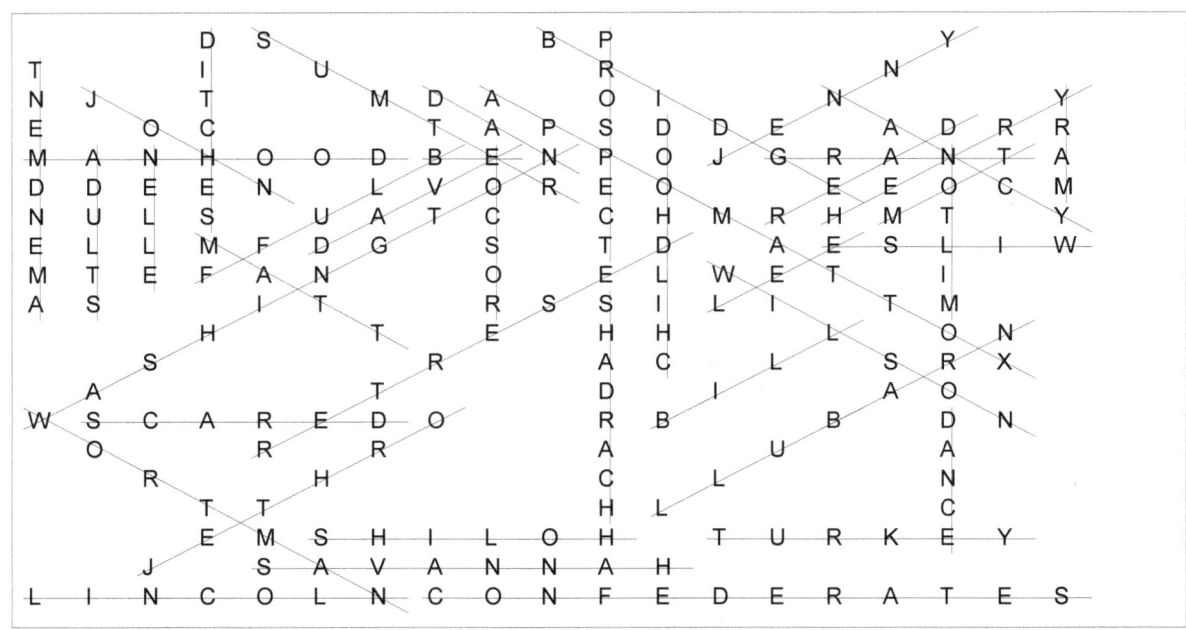

Call Eb used in the woods (6)
Ball's ____ (5)
Bill & he were close brothers who had a fight (4)
Bill told Jethro that being ____ was nothing to be ashamed of (6)
Burdow who rode with Jethro & saved him (4)
Confederates fired on this fort and the war started (6)
Courthouse where the South surrendered (10)
Died on the battlefield (3)
Eb's job was digging these when he rejoined the army (7)
Editor (6)
Ellen gave the letter to Jethro because she could not ____. (4)
Ellen's nephew (5)
Fighters for the South (12)
Jake; wanted Jethro to bring him a newspaper (6)
Jenny went there to see Shad (10)
Jethro considered the victory here to be empty like Pittsburgh landing (6)
Jethro left his behind him in March 1862 (9)
Jethro wrote to Lincoln about his desertion (2)
Jethro's father (4)
Jethro's going to town alone was a step towards his ____. (7)
Jethro's mother (5)
John's wife (5)
Lawrence; Brings news of Tom's death (3)
Married Shad Yale (5)
Mob leader who threatened Jethro (7)
Northern general (5)

People set the Creighton's on fire (4)
Place where Jethro & Dave Burdow were attacked (6)
Point ____; deserters' camp (8)
President during the Civil War (7)
Sherman's gift to Lincoln (8)
Southern general (3)
Teacher (8)
The 13th ____ freed slaves (9)
The union began to win after the fall of Fort ____ in Tennessee (5)
They were troubled by drought, elections, slavery, secession & talk of war (6)
Was killed in an accident (4)
Went to fight for the South (4)
What Eb became by leaving the army (8)
Where Mary had been the night she was killed (5)
Young boy who grew up during the Civil War (6)
____ Run (4)
____'s Creek; battle close to Creighton's home; Union lost (6)

Across Five Aprils Word Search 3

```
A S A V A N N A H O L I H S B B T Y H C
M P M Y W J D H O Y H C H I L D H O O D
P N P Q L U W D R H C Q D G U M X Q Y F
F R N O L S V Y H R A R Q W F M T G K Y
M R O T M D S E T A R E D F N O C E J
Y T S S E A C Z E M D F M X Y B O V W
C K X R P W T N J J A R Q N Y T C Q L Y
P Z A H X E C T X L H V M K G S D R S H
N C X N Y B C F O Z S R A N O F X E N G
S S C B G L S T M X D R N R X Q H V G T
C T S T M N U K V D A L H W K C B Y W R
L Y Y W Y R M L A N N L O W T L Z E R
M I D N K L T V L O C I O I N G B T J J
T B N E L L E M O T E B D E M A R Y N V
T E Y C R N R E T L Y Z M B R E I A A F
J T D R O R V A R I S D B N S R D H N B
P M P S S L M J N M N S J E B E G E C T
W I L S E K N K O E L D D Y U A E N Y H
V I T L L Z M N M H F B A B L D Z R B M
W O R T M A N A R H N G J N L L S Y H T
```

ADULTS	DANCE	LEE	SCARED
AMENDMENT	DAVE	LINCOLN	SHADRACH
APPOMATTOX	DESERTER	MANHOOD	SHILOH
BARN	DITCHES	MARY	SUMTER
BILL	EB	MATT	TOM
BLUFF	ELLEN	MILTON	TURKEY
BRIDGE	GRANT	NANCY	WILSE
BULL	HENRY	PROSPECT	WILSON
CHILDHOOD	JENNY	READ	WORTMAN
CONFEDERATES	JETHRO	ROSCOE	
DAN	JOHN	SAVANNAH	

Across Five Aprils Word Search 3 Answer Key

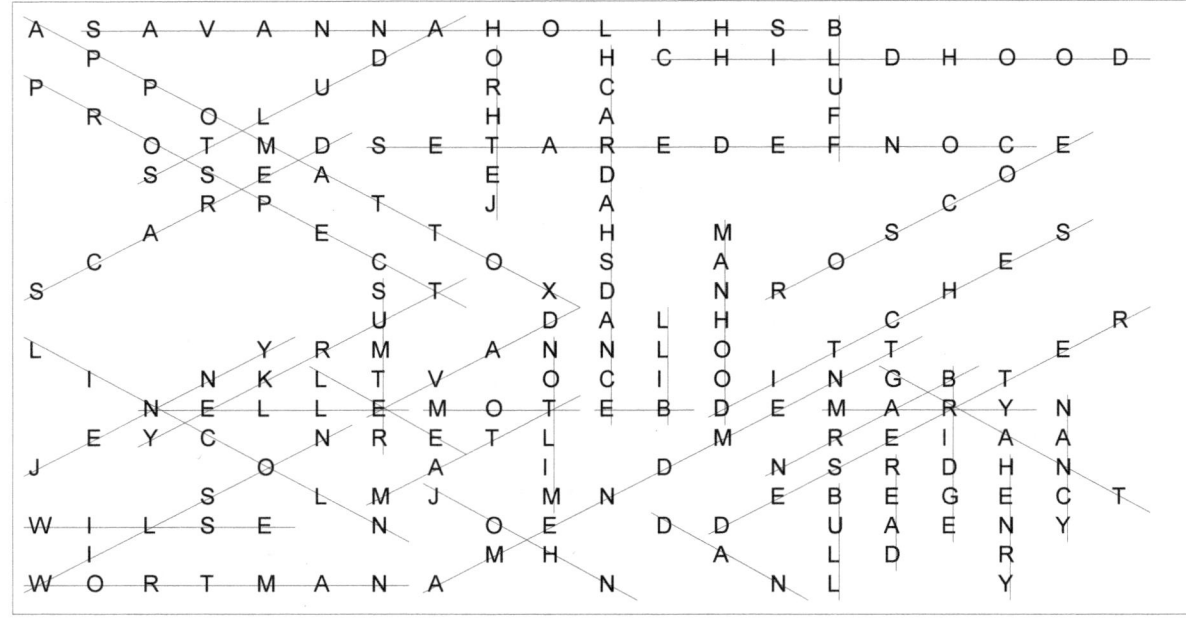

ADULTS	DANCE	LEE	SCARED
AMENDMENT	DAVE	LINCOLN	SHADRACH
APPOMATTOX	DESERTER	MANHOOD	SHILOH
BARN	DITCHES	MARY	SUMTER
BILL	EB	MATT	TOM
BLUFF	ELLEN	MILTON	TURKEY
BRIDGE	GRANT	NANCY	WILSE
BULL	HENRY	PROSPECT	WILSON
CHILDHOOD	JENNY	READ	WORTMAN
CONFEDERATES	JETHRO	ROSCOE	
DAN	JOHN	SAVANNAH	

Across Five Aprils Word Search 4

```
A S H I L O H F B Q L Y S W B R N T F V
M M Q V Q A Y Q Z U C G A R K L X N B Y
D H E Y N G D G G N L S V R H V U H Z T
K E W N V Q S U A W H A L J S S F Y K
D F S H D R Q N L I R N N D L Y R R F Y
R Q F E D M V J N T A T N W F E Y T V W
N B Z C R Q E G V M S C A S T K L G D S
W V M X R T T N T G S E H M T R S G K S
W C B D M O E R T S E P U R B U V J G N
K A O C N G O R B X H S Q O F T P D Z Q
J P F N V W W P Y S C O Q S N Y R W S F
T P R T F H H G H H T R C C R T E Q E Q
N O Q Y W E Y A L K I P D O A K A G H B
N M C H I L D H O O D A V E B D D N W Q
V A M W K R X E Y E Y S E B O I L I F J
W T J G A C T P R N L L D O R O L M G X
I T O C S N Y A N A N L H B C S Y L X R
L O H D A N C E E T T N E N O R H T E J
S X N R A S J K H O A E I N A N N M Z Z
E X G D M A T T M M L S M I L T O N V
```

ADULTS	DANCE	LEE	SCARED
AMENDMENT	DAVE	LINCOLN	SHADRACH
APPOMATTOX	DESERTER	MANHOOD	SHILOH
BARN	DITCHES	MARY	SUMTER
BILL	EB	MATT	TOM
BLUFF	ELLEN	MILTON	TURKEY
BRIDGE	GRANT	NANCY	WASHINGTON
BULL	HENRY	PROSPECT	WILSE
CHILDHOOD	JENNY	READ	WILSON
CONFEDERATES	JETHRO	ROSCOE	WORTMAN
DAN	JOHN	SAVANNAH	

Across Five Aprils Word Search 4 Answer Key

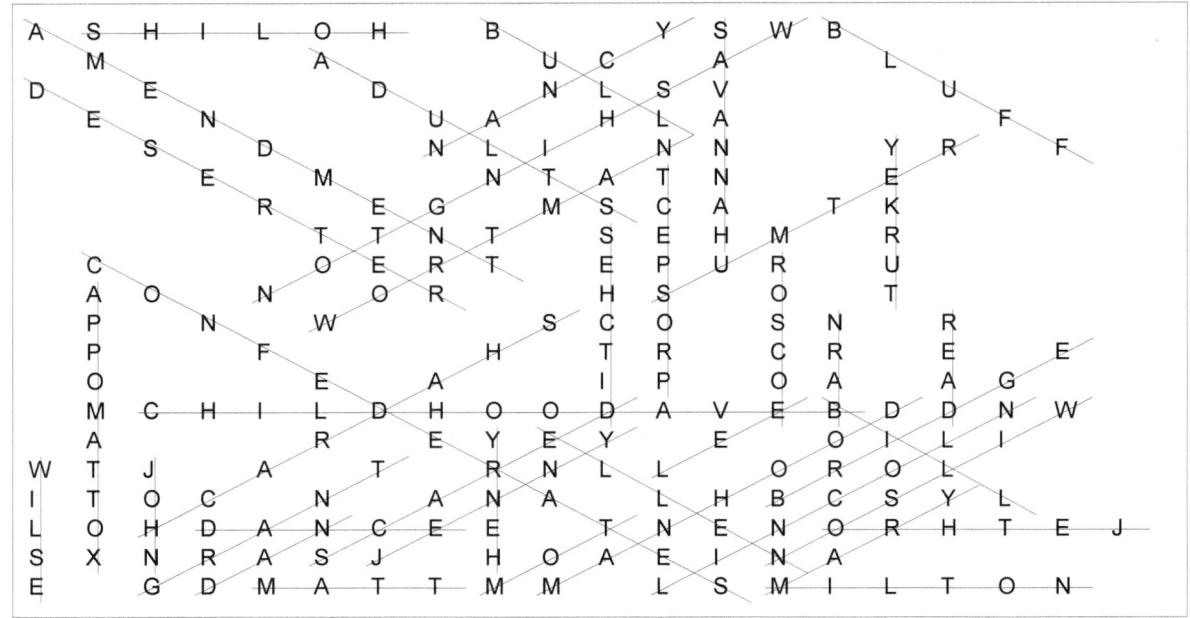

ADULTS	DANCE	LEE	SCARED
AMENDMENT	DAVE	LINCOLN	SHADRACH
APPOMATTOX	DESERTER	MANHOOD	SHILOH
BARN	DITCHES	MARY	SUMTER
BILL	EB	MATT	TOM
BLUFF	ELLEN	MILTON	TURKEY
BRIDGE	GRANT	NANCY	WASHINGTON
BULL	HENRY	PROSPECT	WILSE
CHILDHOOD	JENNY	READ	WILSON
CONFEDERATES	JETHRO	ROSCOE	WORTMAN
DAN	JOHN	SAVANNAH	

Across Five Aprils Crossword 1

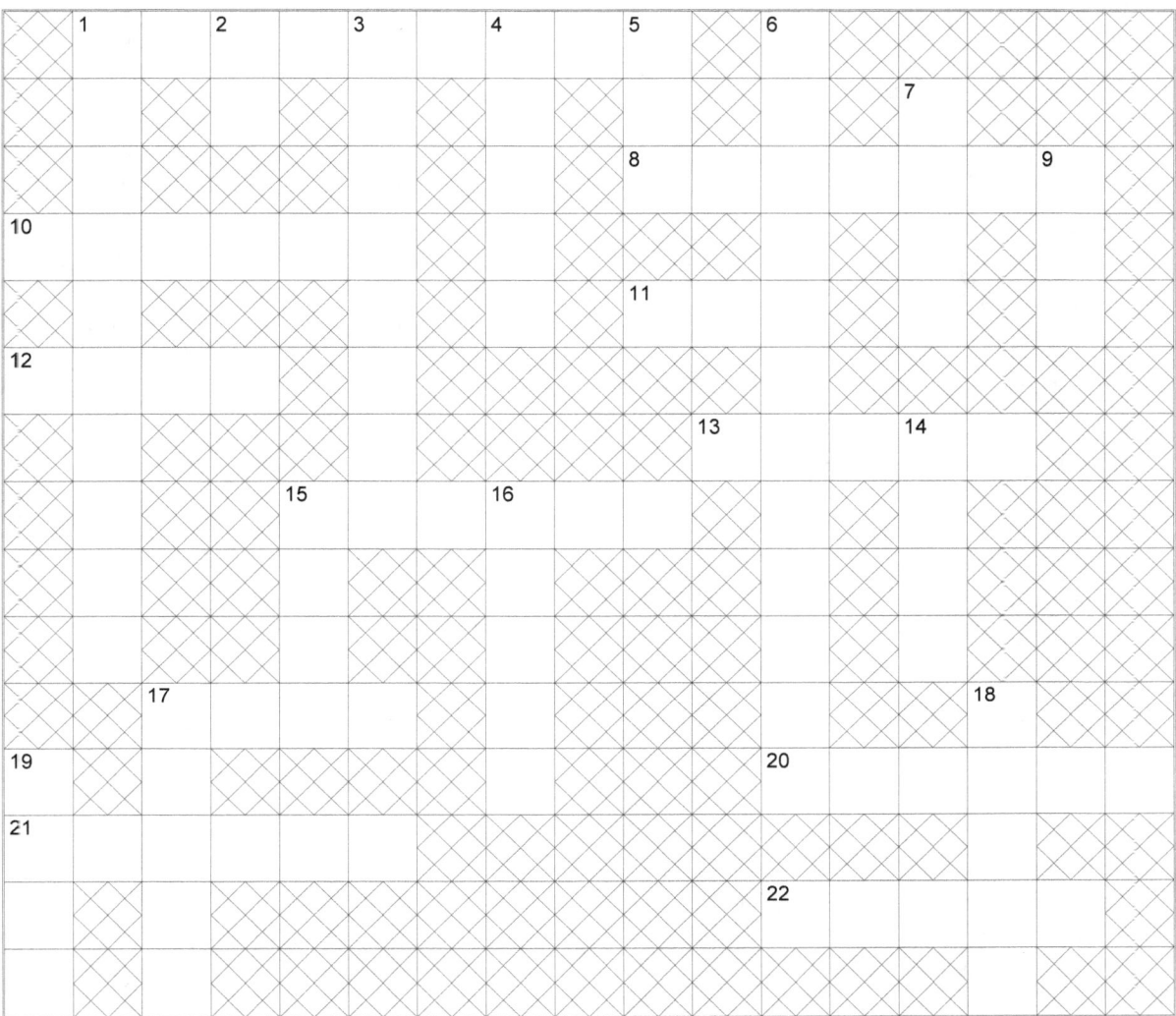

Across
1. The 13th ____ freed slaves
3. Jethro's going to town alone was a step towards his ____.
10. Jake; wanted Jethro to bring him a newspaper
11. Southern general
12. Burdow who rode with Jethro & saved him
13. The union began to win after the fall of Fort ____ in Tennessee
15. Place where Jethro & Dave Burdow were attacked
17. Went to fight for the South
20. Bill told Jethro that being ____ was nothing to be ashamed of
21. They were troubled by drought, elections, slavery, secession & talk of war
22. Married Shad Yale

Down
1. Courthouse where the South surrendered
2. Jethro wrote to Lincoln about his desertion
3. What Eb became by leaving the army
4. Jethro's mother
5. Died on the battlefield
6. Fighters for the South
7. Bill & he were close brothers who had a fight
9. Lawrence; Brings news of Tom's death
14. Ellen gave the letter to Jethro because she could not ____.
15. ____ Run
16. Where Mary had been the night she was killed
17. Ball's ____
18. Northern general
19. People set the Creighton's on fire

Across Five Aprils Crossword 1 Answer Key

	1		2		3		4		5		6			
	A	M	E	N	D	M	E	N	T		C			
	P		B		E		L		O		O		7	
													J	
	P				S		L		8 M	A	N	H	O	O	9 D
10 R	O	S	C	O	E		E				F		H		A
	M					R		N		11 L	E	E		N		N
12 D	A	V	E			T						D			
	T					E				13 H	E	N	14 R	Y	
	T			15 B	R	I	16 D	G	E		R		E		
	O			U			A				A		A		
	X			L			N				T		D		
		17 B	I	L	L		C				E		18 G		
19 B	L						E			20 S	C	A	R	E	D
21 A	D	U	L	T	S								A		
R	F									22 J	E	N	N	Y	
N	F												T		

Across
1. The 13th ____ freed slaves
8. Jethro's going to town alone was a step towards his ____.
10. Jake; wanted Jethro to bring him a newspaper
11. Southern general
12. Burdow who rode with Jethro & saved him
13. The union began to win after the fall of Fort ____ in Tennessee
15. Place where Jethro & Dave Burdow were attacked
17. Went to fight for the South
20. Bill told Jethro that being ____ was nothing to be ashamed of
21. They were troubled by drought, elections, slavery, secession & talk of war
22. Married Shad Yale

Down
1. Courthouse where the South surrendered
2. Jethro wrote to Lincoln about his desertion
3. What Eb became by leaving the army
4. Jethro's mother
5. Died on the battlefield
6. Fighters for the South
7. Bill & he were close brothers who had a fight
9. Lawrence; Brings news of Tom's death
14. Ellen gave the letter to Jethro because she could not ____.
15. ____ Run
16. Where Mary had been the night she was killed
17. Ball's ____
18. Northern general
19. People set the Creighton's on fire

Across Five Aprils Crossword 2

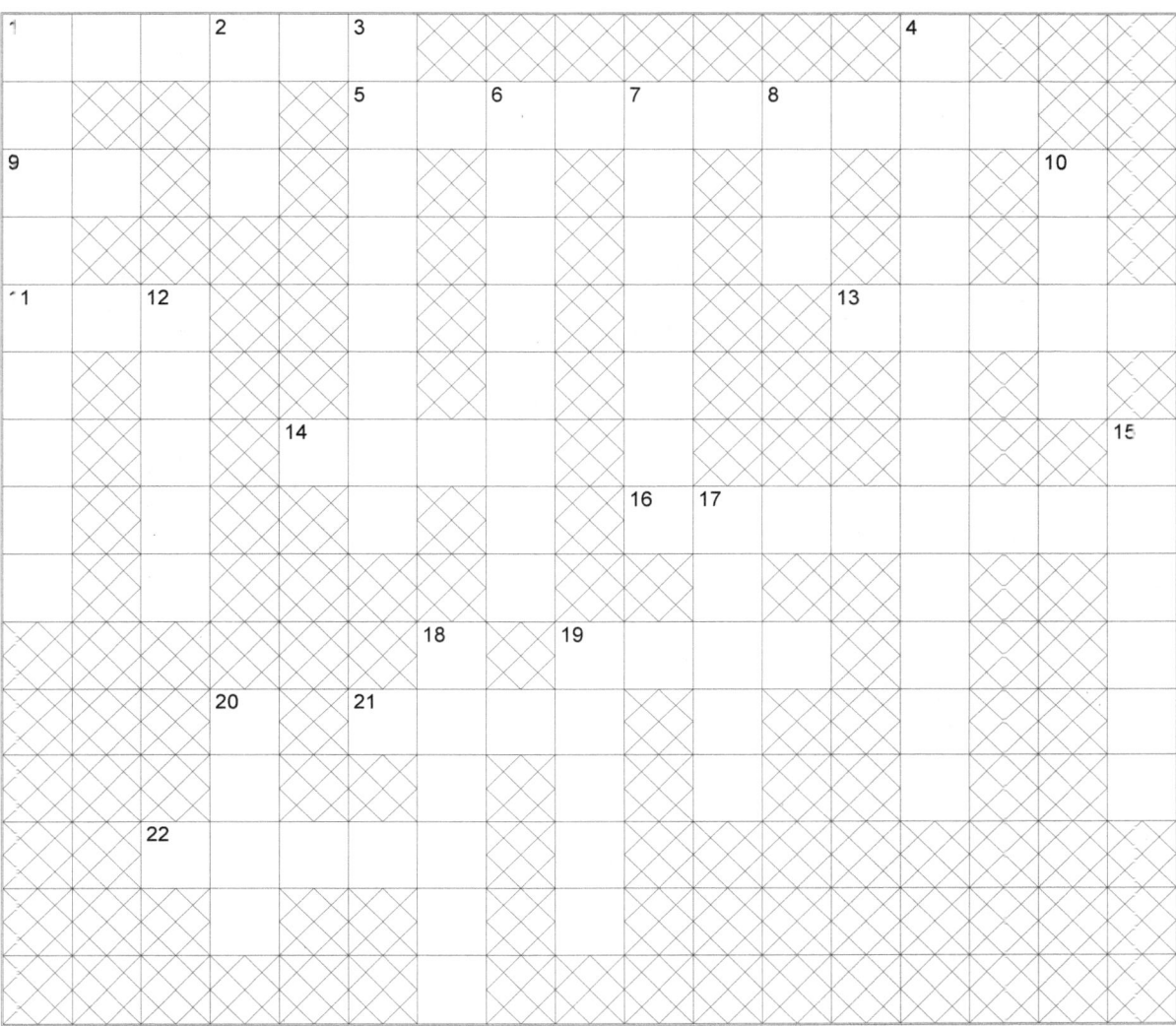

Across
1. They were troubled by drought, elections, slavery, secession & talk of war
5. Courthouse where the South surrendered
9. Jethro wrote to Lincoln about his desertion
11. Lawrence; Brings news of Tom's death
13. The union began to win after the fall of Fort ____ in Tennessee
14. Burdow who rode with Jethro & saved him
16. What Eb became by leaving the army
19. Went to fight for the South
21. ____ Run
22. Northern general

Down
1. The 13th ____ freed slaves
2. Southern general
3. Sherman's gift to Lincoln
4. Fighters for the South
6. Point ____; deserters' camp
7. Jethro's going to town alone was a step towards his ____.
8. Died on the battlefield
10. People set the Creighton's on fire
12. John's wife
15. Place where Jethro & Dave Burdow were attacked
17. Jethro's mother
18. Confederates fired on this fort and the war started
19. Ball's ____
20. Was killed in an accident

Across Five Aprils Crossword 2 Answer Key

	1 A	D	2 U	L	3 T	S					4 C		
	M		E		5 A	P	6 P	7 O	M	8 T	T	O	X
	9 E	B			E	V	R	A	O		N		10 B
	N				A		O	N		M	F		A
	11 D	A	12 N			N		S		H	13 E	N	R	Y
	M		A			N		P		O		D		N
	E		N	14 D	A	V	E			O		E		15 B
	N		C		A		C	16 D	17 E	S	E	R	T	E	R
	T		Y		H		T		L			A		I
						18 S		19 B	I	L	L		T		D
				20 M		21 B	U	L	L		E		E		G
				A			M		U		N		S		E
			22 G	R	A	N	T		F					
				Y			E		F					
							R						

Across
1. They were troubled by drought, elections, slavery, secession & talk of war
5. Courthouse where the South surrendered
9. Jethro wrote to Lincoln about his desertion
11. Lawrence; Brings news of Tom's death
13. The union began to win after the fall of Fort ____ in Tennessee
14. Burdow who rode with Jethro & saved him
16. What Eb became by leaving the army
19. Went to fight for the South
21. ____ Run
22. Northern general

Down
1. The 13th ____ freed slaves
2. Southern general
3. Sherman's gift to Lincoln
4. Fighters for the South
6. Point ____; deserters' camp
7. Jethro's going to town alone was a step towards his ____.
8. Died on the battlefield
10. People set the Creighton's on fire
12. John's wife
15. Place where Jethro & Dave Burdow were attacked
17. Jethro's mother
18. Confederates fired on this fort and the war started
19. Ball's ____
20. Was killed in an accident

Across Five Aprils Crossword 3

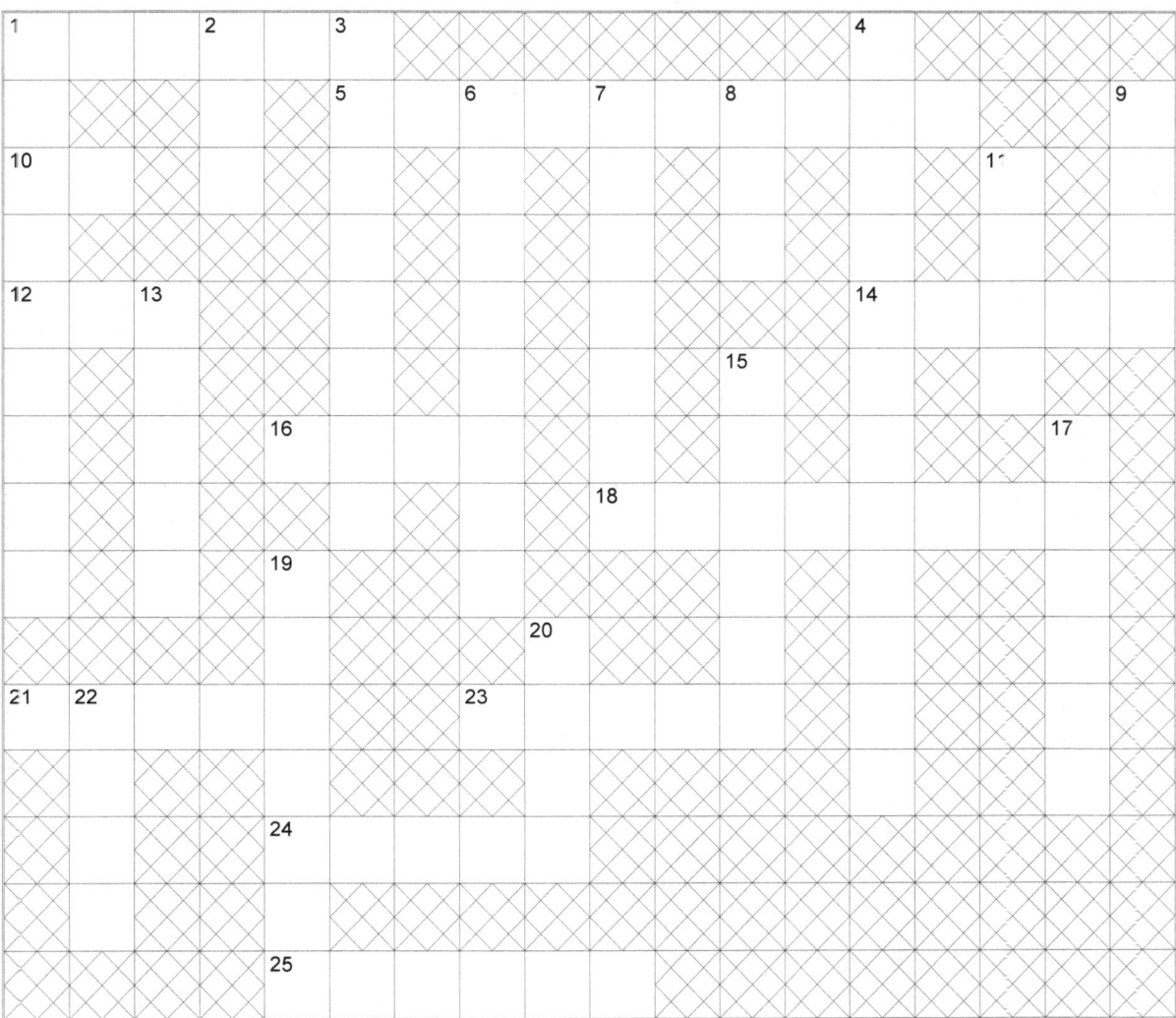

Across
1. They were troubled by drought, elections, slavery, secession & talk of war
5. Courthouse where the South surrendered
10. Jethro wrote to Lincoln about his desertion
12. Lawrence; Brings news of Tom's death
14. Jethro's mother
16. Burdow who rode with Jethro & saved him
18. What Eb became by leaving the army
21. Northern general
23. Where Mary had been the night she was killed
24. The union began to win after the fall of Fort ____ in Tennessee
25. Bill told Jethro that being ____ was nothing to be ashamed of

Down
1. The 13th ____ freed slaves
2. Southern general
3. Sherman's gift to Lincoln
4. Fighters for the South
6. Point ____; deserters' camp
7. Jethro's going to town alone was a step towards his ____.
8. Died on the battlefield
9. People set the Creighton's on fire
11. Went to fight for the South
13. John's wife
15. Jake; wanted Jethro to bring him a newspaper
17. Place where Jethro & Dave Burdow were attacked
19. Eb's job was digging these when he rejoined the army
20. Was killed in an accident
22. Ellen gave the letter to Jethro because she could not ____.

Across Five Aprils Crossword 3 Answer Key

¹A	D	²U	L	³T	S				⁴C	
M		E		⁵A	⁶P	⁷P	⁸O	M	A	T	T	O	X		⁹B
¹⁰E	B	E		V		R	A	O	N		¹¹B	A
N				A		O	N	M	F		I	R
¹²D	A	¹³N		N	S	H		¹⁴E	L	L	E	N
M		A		N	P	O	¹⁵R	D	L	
E		¹⁶D	A	V	E	O	O	E		¹⁷B
N	C	H	C	¹⁸D	E	S	E	R	T	E	R
T	Y	¹⁹D		T		C	A		I
		I			²⁰M		O	T		D
²¹G	²²R	A	N	T	²³D	A	N	C	E	E	G
	E		C		R		E	S	E
	A	²⁴H	E	N	R	Y
	D		E
		²⁵S	C	A	R	E	D

Across
1. They were troubled by drought, elections, slavery, secession & talk of war
5. Courthouse where the South surrendered
10. Jethro wrote to Lincoln about his desertion
12. Lawrence; Brings news of Tom's death
14. Jethro's mother
16. Burdow who rode with Jethro & saved him
18. What Eb became by leaving the army
21. Northern general
23. Where Mary had been the night she was killed
24. The union began to win after the fall of Fort ____ in Tennessee
25. Bill told Jethro that being ____ was nothing to be ashamed of

Down
1. The 13th ____ freed slaves
2. Southern general
3. Sherman's gift to Lincoln
4. Fighters for the South
6. Point ____; deserters' camp
7. Jethro's going to town alone was a step towards his ____.
8. Died on the battlefield
9. People set the Creighton's on fire
11. Went to fight for the South
13. John's wife
15. Jake; wanted Jethro to bring him a newspaper
17. Place where Jethro & Dave Burdow were attacked
19. Eb's job was digging these when he rejoined the army
20. Was killed in an accident
22. Ellen gave the letter to Jethro because she could not ____.

Across Five Aprils Crossword 4

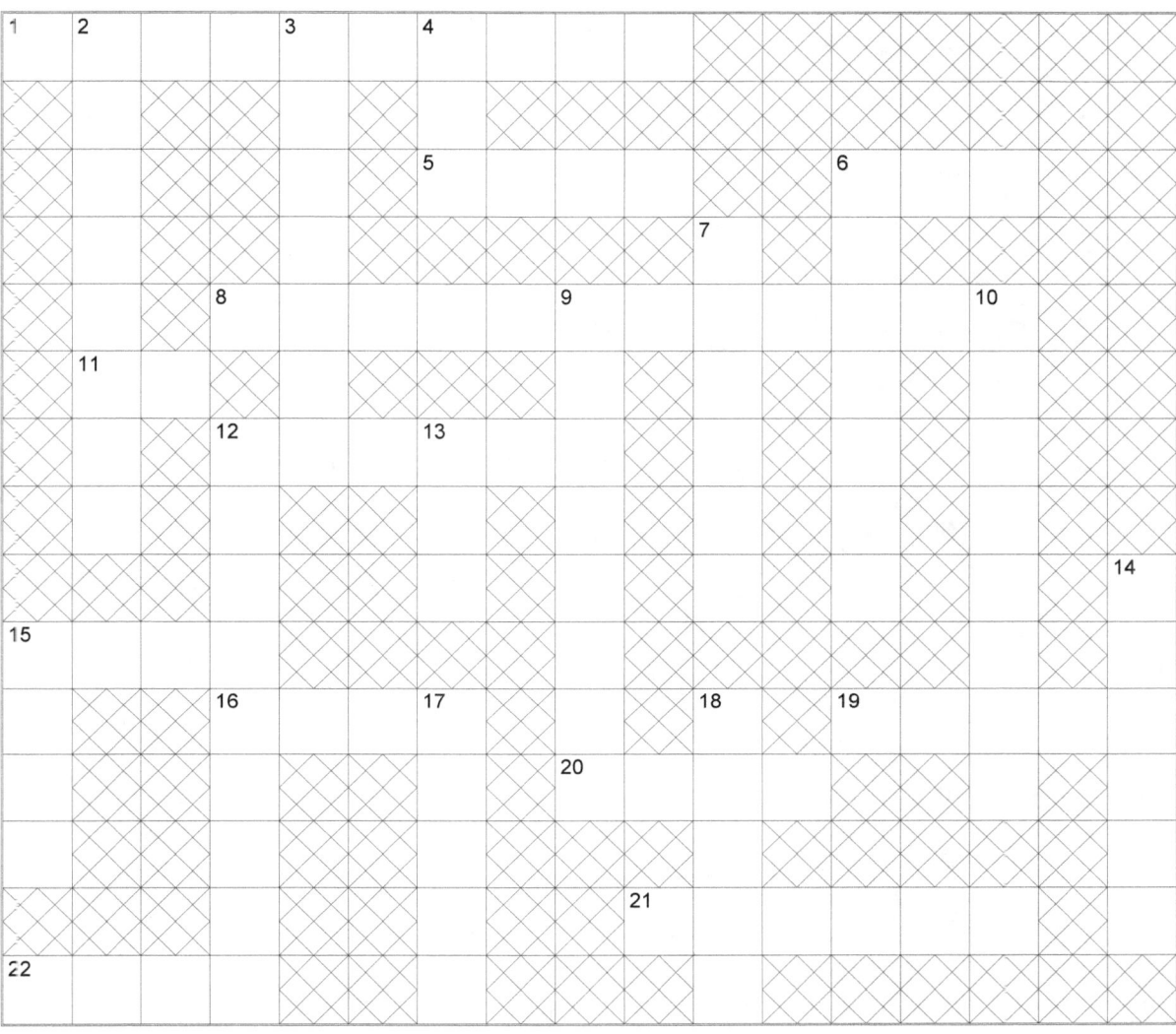

Across
1. Courthouse where the South surrendered
5. Was killed in an accident
6. Lawrence; Brings news of Tom's death
8. Fighters for the South
11. Jethro wrote to Lincoln about his desertion
12. They were troubled by drought, elections, slavery, secession & talk of war
15. People set the Creighton's on fire
16. Burdow who rode with Jethro & saved him
19. Northern general
20. Ellen gave the letter to Jethro because she could not ____.
21. Bill told Jethro that being ____ was nothing to be ashamed of
22. Jethro's father

Down
2. Point ____; deserters' camp
3. Jethro's going to town alone was a step towards his ____.
4. Died on the battlefield
6. Eb's job was digging these when he rejoined the army
7. Place where Jethro & Dave Burdow were attacked
9. What Eb became by leaving the army
10. Sherman's gift to Lincoln
12. The 13th ____ freed slaves
13. Southern general
14. Young boy who grew up during the Civil War
15. Went to fight for the South
17. Jethro's mother
18. Where Mary had been the night she was killed

Across Five Aprils Crossword 4 Answer Key

	1 A	2 P	P	3 O	M	4 A	T	T	O	X			
		R		A		O							
		O		N		5 M	A	R	Y		6 D	A	N
		S		H				7 B		I			
		P		8 C	O	N	F	9 E	D	E	R	A	T	E	10 S
	11 E	B		O				E		I		C		A
	C		12 A	D	U	13 L	T	S		D		H		V
	T		M			E		E		G		E		A
			E			E		R		E		S		N	14 J
15 B	A	R	N					T						N	E
I			16 D	A	V	17 E		18 D		19 G	R	A	N	T
L			M			L		20 R	E	A	D			H	H
L			E			L		N							R
			N			E		21 S	C	A	R	E	D		O
22 M	A	T	T			N		E							

Across
1. Courthouse where the South surrendered
5. Was killed in an accident
6. Lawrence; Brings news of Tom's death
8. Fighters for the South
11. Jethro wrote to Lincoln about his desertion
12. They were troubled by drought, elections, slavery, secession & talk of war
15. People set the Creighton's on fire
16. Burdow who rode with Jethro & saved him
19. Northern general
20. Ellen gave the letter to Jethro because she could not ____.
21. Bill told Jethro that being ____ was nothing to be ashamed of
22. Jethro's father

Down
2. Point ____; deserters' camp
3. Jethro's going to town alone was a step towards his ____.
4. Died on the battlefield
6. Eb's job was digging these when he rejoined the army
7. Place where Jethro & Dave Burdow were attacked
9. What Eb became by leaving the army
10. Sherman's gift to Lincoln
12. The 13th ____ freed slaves
13. Southern general
14. Young boy who grew up during the Civil War
15. Went to fight for the South
17. Jethro's mother
18. Where Mary had been the night she was killed

Across Five Aprils

AMENDMENT	SHILOH	ELLEN	TOM	CONFEDERATES
APPOMATTOX	WILSE	DITCHES	BLUFF	SUMTER
LEE	NANCY	FREE SPACE	WASHINGTON	SCARED
MILTON	DANCE	JETHRO	MATT	LINCOLN
GRANT	ADULTS	BRIDGE	SHADRACH	BARN

Across Five Aprils

SAVANNAH	MARY	TURKEY	DAVE	BILL
PROSPECT	DESERTER	CHILDHOOD	JOHN	WILSON
EB	READ	FREE SPACE	DAN	WORTMAN
HENRY	BULL	JENNY	BARN	SHADRACH
BRIDGE	ADULTS	GRANT	LINCOLN	MATT

Across Five Aprils

LEE	JENNY	SCARED	GRANT	BRIDGE
ROSCOE	MATT	BILL	EB	WILSE
JETHRO	CONFEDERATES	FREE SPACE	JOHN	READ
DANCE	DAN	MILTON	WILSON	SAVANNAH
ADULTS	WASHINGTON	AMENDMENT	SHADRACH	DAVE

Across Five Aprils

TOM	SUMTER	BARN	BULL	DESERTER
DITCHES	LINCOLN	APPOMATTOX	TURKEY	SHILOH
NANCY	MANHOOD	FREE SPACE	BLUFF	CHILDHOOD
PROSPECT	HENRY	WORTMAN	DAVE	SHADRACH
AMENDMENT	WASHINGTON	ADULTS	SAVANNAH	WILSON

Across Five Aprils

TURKEY	AMENDMENT	SUMTER	CHILDHOOD	PROSPECT
JENNY	SHILOH	BARN	BLUFF	ADULTS
LEE	CONFEDERATES	FREE SPACE	NANCY	BRIDGE
WASHINGTON	WILSON	LINCOLN	JETHRO	DAVE
DESERTER	SHADRACH	GRANT	JOHN	TOM

Across Five Aprils

APPOMATTOX	READ	MARY	BILL	MANHOOD
ELLEN	WILSE	SCARED	HENRY	MILTON
MATT	DAN	FREE SPACE	DANCE	ROSCOE
EB	SAVANNAH	WORTMAN	TOM	JOHN
GRANT	SHADRACH	DESERTER	DAVE	JETHRO

Across Five Aprils

JENNY	ELLEN	DAN	SAVANNAH	MARY
READ	JETHRO	EB	BRIDGE	DITCHES
JOHN	WILSON	FREE SPACE	MILTON	BULL
NANCY	SHADRACH	LINCOLN	MANHOOD	TURKEY
ROSCOE	MATT	SUMTER	ADULTS	HENRY

Across Five Aprils

BARN	CONFEDERATES	DESERTER	BILL	CHILDHOOD
DAVE	GRANT	LEE	DANCE	WILSE
APPOMATTOX	SHILOH	FREE SPACE	WORTMAN	TOM
AMENDMENT	SCARED	WASHINGTON	HENRY	ADULTS
SUMTER	MATT	ROSCOE	TURKEY	MANHOOD

Across Five Aprils

WILSE	BRIDGE	GRANT	CHILDHOOD	ELLEN
DAVE	EB	SHILOH	DANCE	MARY
SAVANNAH	HENRY	FREE SPACE	WASHINGTON	WILSON
TOM	BLUFF	SHADRACH	MILTON	AMENDMENT
MATT	BILL	DAN	DITCHES	ROSCOE

Across Five Aprils

LEE	DESERTER	WORTMAN	CONFEDERATES	NANCY
JETHRO	BARN	TURKEY	SUMTER	LINCOLN
READ	SCARED	FREE SPACE	BULL	JENNY
ADULTS	JOHN	APPOMATTOX	ROSCOE	DITCHES
DAN	BILL	MATT	AMENDMENT	MILTON

Across Five Aprils

BULL	MATT	SCARED	BILL	TOM
NANCY	JOHN	CHILDHOOD	JETHRO	WILSE
ADULTS	PROSPECT	FREE SPACE	DAVE	WORTMAN
ROSCOE	BARN	DITCHES	BRIDGE	AMENDMENT
GRANT	DAN	SUMTER	WASHINGTON	READ

Across Five Aprils

DANCE	MARY	SAVANNAH	JENNY	EB
DESERTER	CONFEDERATES	APPOMATTOX	SHILOH	MANHOOD
SHADRACH	ELLEN	FREE SPACE	MILTON	TURKEY
LEE	WILSON	BLUFF	READ	WASHINGTON
SUMTER	DAN	GRANT	AMENDMENT	BRIDGE

Across Five Aprils

AMENDMENT	LINCOLN	MARY	SHILOH	CONFEDERATES
SHADRACH	BRIDGE	WORTMAN	EB	TURKEY
PROSPECT	NANCY	FREE SPACE	BILL	WILSE
BARN	BULL	BLUFF	JETHRO	WASHINGTON
DANCE	MANHOOD	DESERTER	SAVANNAH	GRANT

Across Five Aprils

SCARED	HENRY	CHILDHOOD	TOM	SUMTER
READ	DAVE	LEE	JOHN	JENNY
DITCHES	ADULTS	FREE SPACE	APPOMATTOX	ELLEN
DAN	MILTON	MATT	GRANT	SAVANNAH
DESERTER	MANHOOD	DANCE	WASHINGTON	JETHRO

Across Five Aprils

MATT	JENNY	WASHINGTON	SHILOH	BULL
BLUFF	WORTMAN	CONFEDERATES	WILSON	ADULTS
BRIDGE	JOHN	FREE SPACE	TURKEY	SCARED
LEE	EB	SHADRACH	DAN	ELLEN
DAVE	PROSPECT	APPOMATTOX	BILL	CHILDHOOD

Across Five Aprils

NANCY	MILTON	MANHOOD	AMENDMENT	SUMTER
WILSE	GRANT	MARY	DESERTER	TOM
READ	DITCHES	FREE SPACE	SAVANNAH	HENRY
DANCE	BARN	JETHRO	CHILDHOOD	BILL
APPOMATTOX	PROSPECT	DAVE	ELLEN	DAN

Across Five Aprils

APPOMATTOX	LEE	HENRY	MILTON	DANCE
SUMTER	DAN	WASHINGTON	MARY	ADULTS
WILSE	GRANT	FREE SPACE	JENNY	SHILOH
BULL	TURKEY	CONFEDERATES	PROSPECT	AMENDMENT
SHADRACH	DESERTER	MATT	BRIDGE	READ

Across Five Aprils

BARN	MANHOOD	DAVE	ELLEN	JETHRO
SAVANNAH	BLUFF	BILL	WORTMAN	JOHN
DITCHES	LINCOLN	FREE SPACE	CHILDHOOD	ROSCOE
EB	SCARED	NANCY	READ	BRIDGE
MATT	DESERTER	SHADRACH	AMENDMENT	PROSPECT

Across Five Aprils

BRIDGE	DAN	HENRY	NANCY	WILSE
CHILDHOOD	LINCOLN	DANCE	MANHOOD	WORTMAN
AMENDMENT	JOHN	FREE SPACE	MILTON	JETHRO
ROSCOE	SUMTER	TOM	PROSPECT	TURKEY
WASHINGTON	SCARED	JENNY	BARN	BILL

Across Five Aprils

ADULTS	WILSON	ELLEN	DESERTER	DITCHES
APPOMATTOX	EB	LEE	BLUFF	CONFEDERATES
SHILOH	BULL	FREE SPACE	READ	MATT
GRANT	SHADRACH	MARY	BILL	BARN
JENNY	SCARED	WASHINGTON	TURKEY	PROSPECT

Across Five Aprils

MATT	CHILDHOOD	HENRY	DAN	BILL
ELLEN	MILTON	SAVANNAH	SHILOH	TURKEY
DITCHES	SCARED	FREE SPACE	PROSPECT	JENNY
DAVE	DESERTER	BULL	TOM	NANCY
AMENDMENT	BARN	EB	WASHINGTON	MANHOOD

Across Five Aprils

CONFEDERATES	ROSCOE	WILSON	SUMTER	LINCOLN
JOHN	BRIDGE	JETHRO	READ	ADULTS
BLUFF	WORTMAN	FREE SPACE	WILSE	LEE
GRANT	APPOMATTOX	DANCE	MANHOOD	WASHINGTON
EB	BARN	AMENDMENT	NANCY	TOM

Across Five Aprils

SAVANNAH	LINCOLN	MILTON	WORTMAN	ELLEN
MANHOOD	APPOMATTOX	JENNY	SCARED	WASHINGTON
DAVE	TURKEY	FREE SPACE	SUMTER	LEE
PROSPECT	JOHN	BILL	MARY	CHILDHOOD
BRIDGE	BULL	ADULTS	WILSE	JETHRO

Across Five Aprils

WILSON	DESERTER	BLUFF	DAN	SHADRACH
CONFEDERATES	GRANT	ROSCOE	BARN	NANCY
READ	DITCHES	FREE SPACE	SHILOH	TOM
MATT	DANCE	HENRY	JETHRO	WILSE
ADULTS	BULL	BRIDGE	CHILDHOOD	MARY

Across Five Aprils

JENNY	SHILOH	SCARED	WILSON	SUMTER
JETHRO	DESERTER	DAVE	MATT	BARN
ADULTS	LEE	FREE SPACE	GRANT	BLUFF
EB	MARY	NANCY	CONFEDERATES	WASHINGTON
WORTMAN	DITCHES	HENRY	PROSPECT	BRIDGE

Across Five Aprils

TURKEY	ROSCOE	WILSE	BILL	BULL
ELLEN	MILTON	AMENDMENT	READ	CHILDHOOD
TOM	APPOMATTOX	FREE SPACE	DAN	SHADRACH
SAVANNAH	MANHOOD	LINCOLN	BRIDGE	PROSPECT
HENRY	DITCHES	WORTMAN	WASHINGTON	CONFEDERATES

Across Five Aprils

AMENDMENT	SAVANNAH	PROSPECT	DITCHES	DAN
ELLEN	TOM	ROSCOE	SUMTER	WILSON
BLUFF	MANHOOD	FREE SPACE	CONFEDERATES	APPOMATTOX
MATT	MARY	JENNY	ADULTS	BARN
WORTMAN	HENRY	WILSE	DANCE	WASHINGTON

Across Five Aprils

TURKEY	JOHN	NANCY	DAVE	EB
LINCOLN	SCARED	SHILOH	BRIDGE	JETHRO
SHADRACH	DESERTER	FREE SPACE	READ	BULL
BILL	GRANT	CHILDHOOD	WASHINGTON	DANCE
WILSE	HENRY	WORTMAN	BARN	ADULTS

Across Five Aprils

BLUFF	WORTMAN	BILL	WILSE	BULL
ROSCOE	SAVANNAH	WASHINGTON	TURKEY	DAVE
BRIDGE	DESERTER	FREE SPACE	DITCHES	AMENDMENT
LEE	SUMTER	WILSON	EB	GRANT
DAN	MANHOOD	CONFEDERATES	PROSPECT	MILTON

Across Five Aprils

JOHN	APPOMATTOX	BARN	SCARED	SHADRACH
MATT	MARY	ELLEN	NANCY	ADULTS
DANCE	LINCOLN	FREE SPACE	READ	TOM
CHILDHOOD	SHILOH	JETHRO	MILTON	PROSPECT
CONFEDERATES	MANHOOD	DAN	GRANT	EB

Across Five Aprils

DAVE	READ	SCARED	DAN	HENRY
SUMTER	JETHRO	JENNY	MATT	NANCY
ADULTS	SAVANNAH	FREE SPACE	TURKEY	DITCHES
PROSPECT	WILSE	DANCE	SHADRACH	EB
MANHOOD	TOM	BRIDGE	GRANT	LEE

Across Five Aprils

BARN	CONFEDERATES	BULL	ROSCOE	BLUFF
BILL	MILTON	DESERTER	WORTMAN	CHILDHOOD
AMENDMENT	WASHINGTON	FREE SPACE	JOHN	SHILOH
MARY	ELLEN	LINCOLN	LEE	GRANT
BRIDGE	TOM	MANHOOD	EB	SHADRACH

Across Five Aprils Vocabulary Word List

No.	Word	Clue/Definition
1.	ABOLITIONISTS	People who wanted no more slavery
2.	ADMONITIONS	Reprimands
3.	AGONIZINGLY	With great pain or difficult
4.	ALLUSION	Indirect reference
5.	AMENDED	Fixed; corrected
6.	AMIABLE	Good-natured; friendly
7.	ANNEX	An addition or auxiliary building
8.	APATHY	Indifference
9.	ASTUTE	Shrewd; smart concerning one's own affairs
10.	BELLIGERENTLY	Defiantly; in a hostile manner
11.	BROOKED	Tolerated
12.	BUNTING	Strips of material in patriotic colors used for festive decorations
13.	CAUSTICALLY	Capable of burning; in a fiery manner
14.	COMPATRIOTS	People from one's own country or team
15.	CONTAGION	A bad influence; the spreading of an idea
16.	CONTEMPTUOUS	Scornful
17.	CREDENCE	Believability
18.	CULPRITS	People charged with crimes
19.	DEFILED	Polluted
20.	DESPERADO	Desperate outlaw
21.	DISSIPATED	Dispersed; sent or went away
22.	ENDURANCE	Strength over a long period of time
23.	FATIGUE	Being physically or emotionally tired
24.	GAIETY	Festivity; happiness
25.	GANGRENOUS	Having decaying bodily tissues
26.	GENIALLY	Kindly; pleasantly
27.	HARBOR	To shelter
28.	IMMINENCE	The quality of being about to happen
29.	INCOHERENT	Disjointed; not in an orderly manner
30.	INEPT	Incompetent
31.	IRONCLADS	19th century war ships having sides with metal plates as armor
32.	LOATHING	Feeling of repulsion
33.	MAMMOTH	Huge
34.	OMINOUS	Threatening
35.	PANDEMONIUM	Wild uproar
36.	PASSEL	A bunch; many
37.	PERMEATING	Penetrating; spreading throughout
38.	PREOCCUPATION	Something that engrosses the mind
39.	PREPONDERANCE	Majority
40.	PROVENDER	Food for animals
41.	QUAGMIRE	Soft, muddy land
42.	REITERATED	Said or did something repeatedly
43.	REVERBERATION	An echo-like effect
44.	SHUNNED	Deliberately avoided
45.	STARK	Bare; harsh; desolate
46.	TACIT	Unspoken
47.	TENACITY	Holding or sticking to something persistently
48.	TETHERED	Tied with a short rope or string
49.	TUMULT	Agitation of the mind or emotions; a disturbance

Across Five Aprils Vocabulary Word List

No.	Word	Clue/Definition
50.	TYRANNICAL	Oppressively domineering
51.	VINDICTIVENESS	Revengefulness
52.	WANLY	In a way showing one tired or sad
53.	WASTREL	One who wastes things

Across Five Aprils Vocabulary Fill In The Blank 1

1. People who wanted no more slavery
2. Dispersed; sent or went away
3. 19th century war ships having sides with metal plates as armor
4. Polluted
5. Penetrating; spreading throughout
6. Oppressively domineering
7. People from one's own country or team
8. Festivity; happiness
9. Wild uproar
10. Majority
11. An addition or auxiliary building
12. Believability
13. Feeling of repulsion
14. Having decaying bodily tissues
15. Something that engrosses the mind
16. Desperate outlaw
17. Incompetent
18. Bare; harsh; desolate
19. People charged with crimes
20. Being physically or emotionally tired

Across Five Aprils Vocabulary Fill In The Blank 1 Answer Key

ABOLITIONISTS	1. People who wanted no more slavery
DISSIPATED	2. Dispersed; sent or went away
IRONCLADS	3. 19th century war ships having sides with metal plates as armor
DEFILED	4. Polluted
PERMEATING	5. Penetrating; spreading throughout
TYRANNICAL	6. Oppressively domineering
COMPATRIOTS	7. People from one's own country or team
GAIETY	8. Festivity; happiness
PANDEMONIUM	9. Wild uproar
PREPONDERANCE	10. Majority
ANNEX	11. An addition or auxiliary building
CREDENCE	12. Believability
LOATHING	13. Feeling of repulsion
GANGRENOUS	14. Having decaying bodily tissues
PREOCCUPATION	15. Something that engrosses the mind
DESPERADO	16. Desperate outlaw
INEPT	17. Incompetent
STARK	18. Bare; harsh; desolate
CULPRITS	19. People charged with crimes
FATIGUE	20. Being physically or emotionally tired

Across Five Aprils Vocabulary Fill In The Blank 2

_____

1. Deliberately avoided
2. Indifference
3. Feeling of repulsion
4. Good-natured; friendly
5. Defiantly; in a hostile manner
6. Indirect reference
7. Being physically or emotionally tired
8. People who wanted no more slavery
9. Soft, muddy land
10. Majority
11. Fixed; corrected
12. Huge
13. Bare; harsh; desolate
14. Polluted
15. Said or did something repeatedly
16. People charged with crimes
17. Reprimands
18. Strength over a long period of time
19. Desperate outlaw
20. Tied with a short rope or string

Across Five Aprils Vocabulary Fill In The Blank 2 Answer Key

SHUNNED	1. Deliberately avoided
APATHY	2. Indifference
LOATHING	3. Feeling of repulsion
AMIABLE	4. Good-natured; friendly
BELLIGERENTLY	5. Defiantly; in a hostile manner
ALLUSION	6. Indirect reference
FATIGUE	7. Being physically or emotionally tired
ABOLITIONISTS	8. People who wanted no more slavery
QUAGMIRE	9. Soft, muddy land
PREPONDERANCE	10. Majority
AMENDED	11. Fixed; corrected
MAMMOTH	12. Huge
STARK	13. Bare; harsh; desolate
DEFILED	14. Polluted
REITERATED	15. Said or did something repeatedly
CULPRITS	16. People charged with crimes
ADMONITIONS	17. Reprimands
ENDURANCE	18. Strength over a long period of time
DESPERADO	19. Desperate outlaw
TETHERED	20. Tied with a short rope or string

Across Five Aprils Vocabulary Fill In The Blank 3

1. Unspoken
2. One who wastes things
3. Something that engrosses the mind
4. Wild uproar
5. People who wanted no more slavery
6. Dispersed; sent or went away
7. People from one's own country or team
8. An echo-like effect
9. Scornful
10. Feeling of repulsion
11. Believability
12. Revengefulness
13. Fixed; corrected
14. The quality of being about to happen
15. A bunch; many
16. Being physically or emotionally tired
17. Majority
18. Tolerated
19. An addition or auxiliary building
20. Capable of burning; in a fiery manner

Across Five Aprils Vocabulary Fill In The Blank 3 Answer Key

TACIT	1. Unspoken
WASTREL	2. One who wastes things
PREOCCUPATION	3. Something that engrosses the mind
PANDEMONIUM	4. Wild uproar
ABOLITIONISTS	5. People who wanted no more slavery
DISSIPATED	6. Dispersed; sent or went away
COMPATRIOTS	7. People from one's own country or team
REVERBERATION	8. An echo-like effect
CONTEMPTUOUS	9. Scornful
LOATHING	10. Feeling of repulsion
CREDENCE	11. Believability
VINDICTIVENESS	12. Revengefulness
AMENDED	13. Fixed; corrected
IMMINENCE	14. The quality of being about to happen
PASSEL	15. A bunch; many
FATIGUE	16. Being physically or emotionally tired
PREPONDERANCE	17. Majority
BROOKED	18. Tolerated
ANNEX	19. An addition or auxiliary building
CAUSTICALLY	20. Capable of burning; in a fiery manner

Across Five Aprils Vocabulary Fill In The Blank 4

_____ 1. Shrewd; smart concerning one's own affairs
_____ 2. People who wanted no more slavery
_____ 3. Tolerated
_____ 4. Good-natured; friendly
_____ 5. The quality of being about to happen
_____ 6. Fixed; corrected
_____ 7. One who wastes things
_____ 8. Revengefulness
_____ 9. Penetrating; spreading throughout
_____ 10. People from one's own country or team
_____ 11. Reprimands
_____ 12. Huge
_____ 13. Kindly; pleasantly
_____ 14. Wild uproar
_____ 15. Having decaying bodily tissues
_____ 16. Majority
_____ 17. Scornful
_____ 18. Agitation of the mind or emotions; a disturbance
_____ 19. Holding or sticking to something persistently
_____ 20. To shelter

Across Five Aprils Vocabulary Fill In The Blank 4 Answer Key

ASTUTE	1. Shrewd; smart concerning one's own affairs
ABOLITIONISTS	2. People who wanted no more slavery
BROOKED	3. Tolerated
AMIABLE	4. Good-natured; friendly
IMMINENCE	5. The quality of being about to happen
AMENDED	6. Fixed; corrected
WASTREL	7. One who wastes things
VINDICTIVENESS	8. Revengefulness
PERMEATING	9. Penetrating; spreading throughout
COMPATRIOTS	10. People from one's own country or team
ADMONITIONS	11. Reprimands
MAMMOTH	12. Huge
GENIALLY	13. Kindly; pleasantly
PANDEMONIUM	14. Wild uproar
GANGRENOUS	15. Having decaying bodily tissues
PREPONDERANCE	16. Majority
CONTEMPTUOUS	17. Scornful
TUMULT	18. Agitation of the mind or emotions; a disturbance
TENACITY	19. Holding or sticking to something persistently
HARBOR	20. To shelter

Across Five Aprils Vocabulary Matching 1

___ 1. STARK
___ 2. BUNTING
___ 3. CULPRITS
___ 4. INCOHERENT
___ 5. GAIETY
___ 6. DESPERADO
___ 7. PREOCCUPATION
___ 8. TUMULT
___ 9. IMMINENCE
___10. ADMONITIONS
___11. BELLIGERENTLY
___12. MAMMOTH
___13. IRONCLADS
___14. ANNEX
___15. OMINOUS
___16. AGONIZINGLY
___17. GANGRENOUS
___18. TENACITY
___19. WANLY
___20. PERMEATING
___21. CAUSTICALLY
___22. TACIT
___23. QUAGMIRE
___24. BROOKED
___25. INEPT

A. Desperate outlaw
B. Unspoken
C. The quality of being about to happen
D. Strips of material in patriotic colors used for festive decorations
E. 19th century war ships having sides with metal plates as armor
F. Tolerated
G. Threatening
H. With great pain or difficult
I. Penetrating; spreading throughout
J. Agitation of the mind or emotions; a disturbance
K. Festivity; happiness
L. Disjointed; not in an orderly manner
M. Soft, muddy land
N. Defiantly; in a hostile manner
O. Having decaying bodily tissues
P. Huge
Q. Incompetent
R. Capable of burning; in a fiery manner
S. People charged with crimes
T. Bare; harsh; desolate
U. Reprimands
V. In a way showing one tired or sad
W. Holding or sticking to something persistently
X. Something that engrosses the mind
Y. An addition or auxiliary building

Across Five Aprils Vocabulary Matching 1 Answer Key

T - 1.	STARK	A. Desperate outlaw
D - 2.	BUNTING	B. Unspoken
S - 3.	CULPRITS	C. The quality of being about to happen
L - 4.	INCOHERENT	D. Strips of material in patriotic colors used for festive decorations
K - 5.	GAIETY	E. 19th century war ships having sides with metal plates as armor
A - 6.	DESPERADO	F. Tolerated
X - 7.	PREOCCUPATION	G. Threatening
J - 8.	TUMULT	H. With great pain or difficult
C - 9.	IMMINENCE	I. Penetrating; spreading throughout
U - 10.	ADMONITIONS	J. Agitation of the mind or emotions; a disturbance
N - 11.	BELLIGERENTLY	K. Festivity; happiness
P - 12.	MAMMOTH	L. Disjointed; not in an orderly manner
E - 13.	IRONCLADS	M. Soft, muddy land
Y - 14.	ANNEX	N. Defiantly; in a hostile manner
G - 15.	OMINOUS	O. Having decaying bodily tissues
H - 16.	AGONIZINGLY	P. Huge
O - 17.	GANGRENOUS	Q. Incompetent
W - 18.	TENACITY	R. Capable of burning; in a fiery manner
V - 19.	WANLY	S. People charged with crimes
I - 20.	PERMEATING	T. Bare; harsh; desolate
R - 21.	CAUSTICALLY	U. Reprimands
B - 22.	TACIT	V. In a way showing one tired or sad
M - 23.	QUAGMIRE	W. Holding or sticking to something persistently
F - 24.	BROOKED	X. Something that engrosses the mind
Q - 25.	INEPT	Y. An addition or auxiliary building

Across Five Aprils Vocabulary Matching 2

___ 1. ABOLITIONISTS	A. A bad influence; the spreading of an idea
___ 2. IMMINENCE	B. To shelter
___ 3. PREOCCUPATION	C. Threatening
___ 4. CAUSTICALLY	D. With great pain or difficult
___ 5. AMIABLE	E. Indifference
___ 6. WANLY	F. Food for animals
___ 7. WASTREL	G. One who wastes things
___ 8. ALLUSION	H. In a way showing one tired or sad
___ 9. PROVENDER	I. Indirect reference
___ 10. PASSEL	J. Revengefulness
___ 11. AGONIZINGLY	K. Being physically or emotionally tired
___ 12. SHUNNED	L. Something that engrosses the mind
___ 13. CONTAGION	M. A bunch; many
___ 14. CULPRITS	N. The quality of being about to happen
___ 15. HARBOR	O. Agitation of the mind or emotions; a disturbance
___ 16. VINDICTIVENESS	P. Shrewd; smart concerning one's own affairs
___ 17. AMENDED	Q. Strips of material in patriotic colors used for festive decorations
___ 18. OMINOUS	R. Good-natured; friendly
___ 19. BUNTING	S. Fixed; corrected
___ 20. PREPONDERANCE	T. People charged with crimes
___ 21. APATHY	U. Majority
___ 22. ASTUTE	V. Capable of burning; in a fiery manner
___ 23. TUMULT	W. Deliberately avoided
___ 24. FATIGUE	X. Disjointed; not in an orderly manner
___ 25. INCOHERENT	Y. People who wanted no more slavery

Across Five Aprils Vocabulary Matching 2 Answer Key

Y - 1. ABOLITIONISTS	A. A bad influence; the spreading of an idea
N - 2. IMMINENCE	B. To shelter
L - 3. PREOCCUPATION	C. Threatening
V - 4. CAUSTICALLY	D. With great pain or difficult
R - 5. AMIABLE	E. Indifference
H - 6. WANLY	F. Food for animals
G - 7. WASTREL	G. One who wastes things
I - 8. ALLUSION	H. In a way showing one tired or sad
F - 9. PROVENDER	I. Indirect reference
M - 10. PASSEL	J. Revengefulness
D - 11. AGONIZINGLY	K. Being physically or emotionally tired
W - 12. SHUNNED	L. Something that engrosses the mind
A - 13. CONTAGION	M. A bunch; many
T - 14. CULPRITS	N. The quality of being about to happen
B - 15. HARBOR	O. Agitation of the mind or emotions; a disturbance
J - 16. VINDICTIVENESS	P. Shrewd; smart concerning one's own affairs
S - 17. AMENDED	Q. Strips of material in patriotic colors used for festive decorations
C - 18. OMINOUS	R. Good-natured; friendly
Q - 19. BUNTING	S. Fixed; corrected
U - 20. PREPONDERANCE	T. People charged with crimes
E - 21. APATHY	U. Majority
P - 22. ASTUTE	V. Capable of burning; in a fiery manner
O - 23. TUMULT	W. Deliberately avoided
K - 24. FATIGUE	X. Disjointed; not in an orderly manner
X - 25. INCOHERENT	Y. People who wanted no more slavery

Across Five Aprils Vocabulary Matching 3

___ 1. DESPERADO
___ 2. PREPONDERANCE
___ 3. PASSEL
___ 4. ENDURANCE
___ 5. DEFILED
___ 6. REITERATED
___ 7. TACIT
___ 8. PREOCCUPATION
___ 9. AMENDED
___ 10. CONTEMPTUOUS
___ 11. GANGRENOUS
___ 12. CAUSTICALLY
___ 13. AGONIZINGLY
___ 14. ADMONITIONS
___ 15. ANNEX
___ 16. SHUNNED
___ 17. ABOLITIONISTS
___ 18. ASTUTE
___ 19. BUNTING
___ 20. GENIALLY
___ 21. IMMINENCE
___ 22. STARK
___ 23. CREDENCE
___ 24. MAMMOTH
___ 25. TYRANNICAL

A. Kindly; pleasantly
B. Desperate outlaw
C. With great pain or difficult
D. Oppressively domineering
E. Bare; harsh; desolate
F. Shrewd; smart concerning one's own affairs
G. An addition or auxiliary building
H. The quality of being about to happen
I. Unspoken
J. Strips of material in patriotic colors used for festive decorations
K. Strength over a long period of time
L. People who wanted no more slavery
M. Deliberately avoided
N. Majority
O. Having decaying bodily tissues
P. Something that engrosses the mind
Q. Believability
R. Scornful
S. Reprimands
T. Polluted
U. A bunch; many
V. Huge
W. Capable of burning; in a fiery manner
X. Said or did something repeatedly
Y. Fixed; corrected

Across Five Aprils Vocabulary Matching 3 Answer Key

B - 1. DESPERADO	A.	Kindly; pleasantly
N - 2. PREPONDERANCE	B.	Desperate outlaw
U - 3. PASSEL	C.	With great pain or difficult
K - 4. ENDURANCE	D.	Oppressively domineering
T - 5. DEFILED	E.	Bare; harsh; desolate
X - 6. REITERATED	F.	Shrewd; smart concerning one's own affairs
I - 7. TACIT	G.	An addition or auxiliary building
P - 8. PREOCCUPATION	H.	The quality of being about to happen
Y - 9. AMENDED	I.	Unspoken
R -10. CONTEMPTUOUS	J.	Strips of material in patriotic colors used for festive decorations
O -11. GANGRENOUS	K.	Strength over a long period of time
W -12. CAUSTICALLY	L.	People who wanted no more slavery
C -13. AGONIZINGLY	M.	Deliberately avoided
S -14. ADMONITIONS	N.	Majority
G -15. ANNEX	O.	Having decaying bodily tissues
M -16. SHUNNED	P.	Something that engrosses the mind
L -17. ABOLITIONISTS	Q.	Believability
F -18. ASTUTE	R.	Scornful
J -19. BUNTING	S.	Reprimands
A -20. GENIALLY	T.	Polluted
H -21. IMMINENCE	U.	A bunch; many
E -22. STARK	V.	Huge
Q -23. CREDENCE	W.	Capable of burning; in a fiery manner
V -24. MAMMOTH	X.	Said or did something repeatedly
D -25. TYRANNICAL	Y.	Fixed; corrected

Across Five Aprils Vocabulary Matching 4

___ 1. PERMEATING   A. Kindly; pleasantly
___ 2. PREPONDERANCE   B. Majority
___ 3. TUMULT   C. Agitation of the mind or emotions; a disturbance
___ 4. GENIALLY   D. Revengefulness
___ 5. CULPRITS   E. Dispersed; sent or went away
___ 6. WASTREL   F. Penetrating; spreading throughout
___ 7. MAMMOTH   G. Feeling of repulsion
___ 8. ADMONITIONS   H. Bare; harsh; desolate
___ 9. ASTUTE   I. Defiantly; in a hostile manner
___10. TYRANNICAL   J. People charged with crimes
___11. HARBOR   K. Reprimands
___12. LOATHING   L. Shrewd; smart concerning one's own affairs
___13. DISSIPATED   M. People from one's own country or team
___14. ENDURANCE   N. An addition or auxiliary building
___15. VINDICTIVENESS O. Strength over a long period of time
___16. STARK   P. Incompetent
___17. COMPATRIOTS   Q. Something that engrosses the mind
___18. PREOCCUPATION   R. Indifference
___19. ANNEX   S. Huge
___20. AMIABLE   T. Oppressively domineering
___21. INEPT   U. Festivity; happiness
___22. BELLIGERENTLY   V. The quality of being about to happen
___23. IMMINENCE   W. One who wastes things
___24. APATHY   X. Good-natured; friendly
___25. GAIETY   Y. To shelter

Across Five Aprils Vocabulary Matching 4 Answer Key

F - 1.	PERMEATING	A. Kindly; pleasantly
B - 2.	PREPONDERANCE	B. Majority
C - 3.	TUMULT	C. Agitation of the mind or emotions; a disturbance
A - 4.	GENIALLY	D. Revengefulness
J - 5.	CULPRITS	E. Dispersed; sent or went away
W - 6.	WASTREL	F. Penetrating; spreading throughout
S - 7.	MAMMOTH	G. Feeling of repulsion
K - 8.	ADMONITIONS	H. Bare; harsh; desolate
L - 9.	ASTUTE	I. Defiantly; in a hostile manner
T - 10.	TYRANNICAL	J. People charged with crimes
Y - 11.	HARBOR	K. Reprimands
G - 12.	LOATHING	L. Shrewd; smart concerning one's own affairs
E - 13.	DISSIPATED	M. People from one's own country or team
O - 14.	ENDURANCE	N. An addition or auxiliary building
D - 15.	VINDICTIVENESS	O. Strength over a long period of time
H - 16.	STARK	P. Incompetent
M - 17.	COMPATRIOTS	Q. Something that engrosses the mind
Q - 18.	PREOCCUPATION	R. Indifference
N - 19.	ANNEX	S. Huge
X - 20.	AMIABLE	T. Oppressively domineering
P - 21.	INEPT	U. Festivity; happiness
I - 22.	BELLIGERENTLY	V. The quality of being about to happen
V - 23.	IMMINENCE	W. One who wastes things
R - 24.	APATHY	X. Good-natured; friendly
U - 25.	GAIETY	Y. To shelter

Across Five Aprils Vocabulary Magic Squares 1

Match the definition with the vocabulary word. Put your answers in the magic squares below. When your answers are correct, all columns and rows will add to the same number.

A. CULPRITS
B. ABOLITIONISTS
C. TETHERED
D. TENACITY
E. VINDICTIVENESS
F. TACIT
G. PREPONDERANCE
H. STARK
I. REITERATED
J. COMPATRIOTS
K. BELLIGERENTLY
L. BROOKED
M. DESPERADO
N. SHUNNED
O. AMENDED
P. GANGRENOUS

1. Bare; harsh; desolate
2. People charged with crimes
3. People who wanted no more slavery
4. Majority
5. People from one's own country or team
6. Fixed; corrected
7. Having decaying bodily tissues
8. Said or did something repeatedly
9. Defiantly; in a hostile manner
10. Deliberately avoided
11. Desperate outlaw
12. Tolerated
13. Revengefulness
14. Holding or sticking to something persistently
15. Tied with a short rope or string
16. Unspoken

A=	B=	C=	D=
E=	F=	G=	H=
I=	J=	K=	L=
M=	N=	O=	P=

Across Five Aprils Vocabulary Magic Squares 1 Answer Key

Match the definition with the vocabulary word. Put your answers in the magic squares below. When your answers are correct, all columns and rows will add to the same number.

A. CULPRITS
B. ABOLITIONISTS
C. TETHERED
D. TENACITY
E. VINDICTIVENESS
F. TACIT
G. PREPONDERANCE
H. STARK
I. REITERATED
J. COMPATRIOTS
K. BELLIGERENTLY
L. BROOKED
M. DESPERADO
N. SHUNNED
O. AMENDED
P. GANGRENOUS

1. Bare; harsh; desolate
2. People charged with crimes
3. People who wanted no more slavery
4. Majority
5. People from one's own country or team
6. Fixed; corrected
7. Having decaying bodily tissues
8. Said or did something repeatedly
9. Defiantly; in a hostile manner
10. Deliberately avoided
11. Desperate outlaw
12. Tolerated
13. Revengefulness
14. Holding or sticking to something persistently
15. Tied with a short rope or string
16. Unspoken

A=2	B=3	C=15	D=14
E=13	F=16	G=4	H=1
I=8	J=5	K=9	L=12
M=11	N=10	O=6	P=7

Across Five Aprils Vocabulary Magic Squares 2

Match the definition with the vocabulary word. Put your answers in the magic squares below. When your answers are correct, all columns and rows will add to the same number.

A. ADMONITIONS
B. ANNEX
C. MAMMOTH
D. AGONIZINGLY
E. PANDEMONIUM
F. PASSEL
G. APATHY
H. TYRANNICAL
I. GANGRENOUS
J. ABOLITIONISTS
K. CAUSTICALLY
L. ALLUSION
M. OMINOUS
N. CONTAGION
O. CREDENCE
P. BELLIGERENTLY

1. A bad influence; the spreading of an idea
2. Indifference
3. Indirect reference
4. Reprimands
5. Capable of burning; in a fiery manner
6. An addition or auxiliary building
7. Threatening
8. Oppressively domineering
9. Wild uproar
10. Defiantly; in a hostile manner
11. Huge
12. People who wanted no more slavery
13. With great pain or difficult
14. Having decaying bodily tissues
15. A bunch; many
16. Believability

A=	B=	C=	D=
E=	F=	G=	H=
I=	J=	K=	L=
M=	N=	O=	P=

Across Five Aprils Vocabulary Magic Squares 2 Answer Key

Match the definition with the vocabulary word. Put your answers in the magic squares below. When your answers are correct, all columns and rows will add to the same number.

A. ADMONITIONS
B. ANNEX
C. MAMMOTH
D. AGONIZINGLY
E. PANDEMONIUM
F. PASSEL
G. APATHY
H. TYRANNICAL
I. GANGRENOUS
J. ABOLITIONISTS
K. CAUSTICALLY
L. ALLUSION
M. OMINOUS
N. CONTAGION
O. CREDENCE
P. BELLIGERENTLY

1. A bad influence; the spreading of an idea
2. Indifference
3. Indirect reference
4. Reprimands
5. Capable of burning; in a fiery manner
6. An addition or auxiliary building
7. Threatening
8. Oppressively domineering
9. Wild uproar
10. Defiantly; in a hostile manner
11. Huge
12. People who wanted no more slavery
13. With great pain or difficult
14. Having decaying bodily tissues
15. A bunch; many
16. Believability

A=4	B=6	C=11	D=13
E=9	F=15	G=2	H=8
I=14	J=12	K=5	L=3
M=7	N=1	O=16	P=10

Across Five Aprils Vocabulary Magic Squares 3

Match the definition with the vocabulary word. Put your answers in the magic squares below. When your answers are correct, all columns and rows will add to the same number.

A. ALLUSION
B. HARBOR
C. BROOKED
D. BELLIGERENTLY
E. PREPONDERANCE
F. BUNTING
G. LOATHING
H. FATIGUE
I. ABOLITIONISTS
J. COMPATRIOTS
K. QUAGMIRE
L. CAUSTICALLY
M. WASTREL
N. ENDURANCE
O. AMIABLE
P. TACIT

1. Being physically or emotionally tired
2. One who wastes things
3. To shelter
4. Soft, muddy land
5. People from one's own country or team
6. Tolerated
7. Unspoken
8. Majority
9. Good-natured; friendly
10. Strips of material in patriotic colors used for festive decorations
11. People who wanted no more slavery
12. Defiantly; in a hostile manner
13. Indirect reference
14. Capable of burning; in a fiery manner
15. Feeling of repulsion
16. Strength over a long period of time

A=	B=	C=	D=
E=	F=	G=	H=
I=	J=	K=	L=
M=	N=	O=	P=

Across Five Aprils Vocabulary Magic Squares 3 Answer Key

Match the definition with the vocabulary word. Put your answers in the magic squares below. When your answers are correct, all columns and rows will add to the same number.

A. ALLUSION
B. HARBOR
C. BROOKED
D. BELLIGERENTLY
E. PREPONDERANCE
F. BUNTING
G. LOATHING
H. FATIGUE
I. ABOLITIONISTS
J. COMPATRIOTS
K. QUAGMIRE
L. CAUSTICALLY
M. WASTREL
N. ENDURANCE
O. AMIABLE
P. TACIT

1. Being physically or emotionally tired
2. One who wastes things
3. To shelter
4. Soft, muddy land
5. People from one's own country or team
6. Tolerated
7. Unspoken
8. Majority
9. Good-natured; friendly
10. Strips of material in patriotic colors used for festive decorations
11. People who wanted no more slavery
12. Defiantly; in a hostile manner
13. Indirect reference
14. Capable of burning; in a fiery manner
15. Feeling of repulsion
16. Strength over a long period of time

A=13	B=3	C=6	D=12
E=8	F=10	G=15	H=1
I=11	J=5	K=4	L=14
M=2	N=16	O=9	P=7

Across Five Aprils Vocabulary Magic Squares 4

Match the definition with the vocabulary word. Put your answers in the magic squares below. When your answers are correct, all columns and rows will add to the same number.

A. AGONIZINGLY
B. AMIABLE
C. ALLUSION
D. TYRANNICAL
E. GENIALLY
F. IRONCLADS
G. INEPT
H. PERMEATING
I. LOATHING
J. CULPRITS
K. PASSEL
L. DISSIPATED
M. CONTEMPTUOUS
N. OMINOUS
O. PREPONDERANCE
P. WANLY

1. Scornful
2. 19th century war ships having sides with metal plates as armor
3. Penetrating; spreading throughout
4. Majority
5. Dispersed; sent or went away
6. Indirect reference
7. With great pain or difficult
8. People charged with crimes
9. A bunch; many
10. Oppressively domineering
11. Good-natured; friendly
12. Feeling of repulsion
13. Threatening
14. Kindly; pleasantly
15. Incompetent
16. In a way showing one tired or sad

A=	B=	C=	D=
E=	F=	G=	H=
I=	J=	K=	L=
M=	N=	O=	P=

Across Five Aprils Vocabulary Magic Squares 4 Answer Key

Match the definition with the vocabulary word. Put your answers in the magic squares below. When your answers are correct, all columns and rows will add to the same number.

A. AGONIZINGLY
B. AMIABLE
C. ALLUSION
D. TYRANNICAL
E. GENIALLY
F. IRONCLADS

G. INEPT
H. PERMEATING
I. LOATHING
J. CULPRITS
K. PASSEL
L. DISSIPATED

M. CONTEMPTUOUS
N. OMINOUS
O. PREPONDERANCE
P. WANLY

1. Scornful
2. 19th century war ships having sides with metal plates as armor
3. Penetrating; spreading throughout
4. Majority
5. Dispersed; sent or went away
6. Indirect reference
7. With great pain or difficult
8. People charged with crimes
9. A bunch; many
10. Oppressively domineering
11. Good-natured; friendly
12. Feeling of repulsion
13. Threatening
14. Kindly; pleasantly
15. Incompetent
16. In a way showing one tired or sad

A=7	B=11	C=6	D=10
E=14	F=2	G=15	H=3
I=12	J=8	K=9	L=5
M=1	N=13	O=4	P=16

Across Five Aprils Vocabulary Word Search 1

```
B E L L I G E R E N T L Y L F X J P R W
O M I N O U S X C N P C G N I H T A O L
C P R O V E N D E R K O D W J K X N Q R
F A K V T H D I M M I N E N C E G D G L
S W U C R E D E N C E T F P P L M E A Q
Y T W S D T G U Y L L A I N E G N M P N
L T A N T G B G M L T G L N D C B O A Z
M Z E R X I M I J E P I E L E J U N T N
G M Q S K Y C T N H E O D T U P N I H Q
A C G R O B R A H W A N L Y S S T U Y T
N T N A D K C F L M A U D D L N I M W C
G Y I S I I H R S L M S A U E P N O S G
R R T W T E S R E U Y L T R R J G T N H
E A A Y N R T S T B C S E R J A I Z E D
N N E S F M S Y I N R H H E E R N L K P
O N M Z G A J J O P O O T U P L B C X F
U I R M P Q Y R J C A U O L N A W D E Z
S C E T A C I T N N T T U K I N L H N G
R A P M X R B I K S Y C E M E K E Z N Q
N L L E R I M G A U Q H A D N D M D A J
```

19th century war ships having sides with metal plates as armor (9)
A bad influence; the spreading of an idea (9)
A bunch; many (6)
Agitation of the mind or emotions; a disturbance (6)
An addition or auxiliary building (5)
Bare; harsh; desolate (5)
Being physically or emotionally tired (7)
Believability (8)
Capable of burning; in a fiery manner (11)
Defiantly; in a hostile manner (13)
Deliberately avoided (7)
Disjointed; not in an orderly manner (10)
Dispersed; sent or went away (10)
Feeling of repulsion (8)
Festivity; happiness (6)
Fixed; corrected (7)
Food for animals (9)
Good-natured; friendly (7)
Having decaying bodily tissues (10)
Holding or sticking to something persistently (8)
In a way showing one tired or sad (5)
Incompetent (5)
Indifference (6)
Indirect reference (8)
Kindly; pleasantly (8)
One who wastes things (7)
Oppressively domineering (10)
Penetrating; spreading throughout (10)
People charged with crimes (8)
Polluted (7)
Shrewd; smart concerning one's own affairs (6)
Soft, muddy land (8)
Strength over a long period of time (9)
Strips of material in patriotic colors used for festive decorations (7)
The quality of being about to happen (9)
Threatening (7)
To shelter (6)
Tolerated (7)
Unspoken (5)
Wild uproar (11)

Across Five Aprils Vocabulary Word Search 1 Answer Key

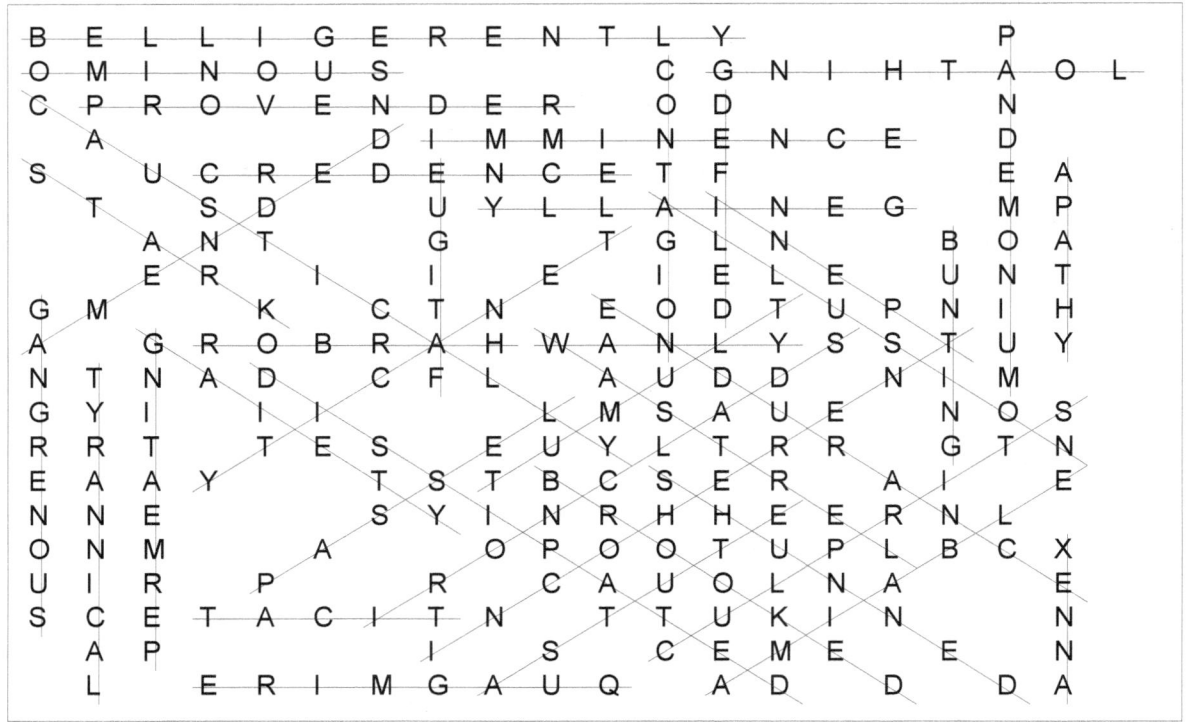

19th century war ships having sides with metal plates as armor (9)
A bad influence; the spreading of an idea (9)
A bunch; many (6)
Agitation of the mind or emotions; a disturbance (6)
An addition or auxiliary building (5)
Bare; harsh; desolate (5)
Being physically or emotionally tired (7)
Believability (8)
Capable of burning; in a fiery manner (11)
Defiantly; in a hostile manner (13)
Deliberately avoided (7)
Disjointed; not in an orderly manner (10)
Dispersed; sent or went away (10)
Feeling of repulsion (8)
Festivity; happiness (6)
Fixed; corrected (7)
Food for animals (9)
Good-natured; friendly (7)
Having decaying bodily tissues (10)
Holding or sticking to something persistently (8)
In a way showing one tired or sad (5)
Incompetent (5)
Indifference (6)
Indirect reference (8)
Kindly; pleasantly (8)
One who wastes things (7)
Oppressively domineering (10)
Penetrating; spreading throughout (10)
People charged with crimes (8)
Polluted (7)
Shrewd; smart concerning one's own affairs (6)
Soft, muddy land (8)
Strength over a long period of time (9)
Strips of material in patriotic colors used for festive decorations (7)
The quality of being about to happen (9)
Threatening (7)
To shelter (6)
Tolerated (7)
Unspoken (5)
Wild uproar (11)

Across Five Aprils Vocabulary Word Search 2

```
C A U S T I C A L L Y L Q H A R B O R B
P A N D E M O N I U M R U B R O O K E D
G E N I A L L Y D D W K A S M Q H X Y G
T D L P J Z S E E F N G G U H K H T N N
E G D S V C R L N I G M O T G P I L C
N C E L D E I T N A R S I N A E H G F V
A K D J H F X E S G U M R I R T A N N L
C O N T E M P T U O U S E M A M M O T H
I O E D Z T A W N N W T E O I E I N Y
T T M W Y R S E L I Y A L A T S P T E N
Y C A P K R R E W Z T Y B U U Z R A R H
D O C N A G R L A I R L T L T E O R E Z
L N D J N T E S N N E S L L U D V E H X
B T Y A S S R G L G A A U G A E E B O J
R A G A S L Q I Y L S M I R T N N R C V
Z G W A A K Q V O Y U T E F T N D E N P
Q I P F N C T Z C T A P F I F U E V I L
R O B U N T I N G F S W C X J H R E R N
P N P R E P O N D E R A N C E S W R M B
R T Y X X M C C D X T A P A T H Y J Q Z
```

A bad influence; the spreading of an idea (9)
A bunch; many (6)
Agitation of the mind or emotions; a disturbance (6)
An addition or auxiliary building (5)
An echo-like effect (13)
Bare; harsh; desolate (5)
Being physically or emotionally tired (7)
Capable of burning; in a fiery manner (11)
Deliberately avoided (7)
Desperate outlaw (9)
Disjointed; not in an orderly manner (10)
Feeling of repulsion (8)
Festivity; happiness (6)
Fixed; corrected (7)
Food for animals (9)
Good-natured; friendly (7)
Having decaying bodily tissues (10)
Holding or sticking to something persistently (8)
Huge (7)
In a way showing one tired or sad (5)
Incompetent (5)

Indifference (6)
Indirect reference (8)
Kindly; pleasantly (8)
Majority (13)
One who wastes things (7)
Penetrating; spreading throughout (10)
People from one's own country or team (11)
Polluted (7)
Scornful (12)
Shrewd; smart concerning one's own affairs (6)
Soft, muddy land (8)
Strips of material in patriotic colors used for festive decorations (7)
Threatening (7)
Tied with a short rope or string (8)
To shelter (6)
Tolerated (7)
Unspoken (5)
Wild uproar (11)
With great pain or difficult (11)

Across Five Aprils Vocabulary Word Search 2 Answer Key

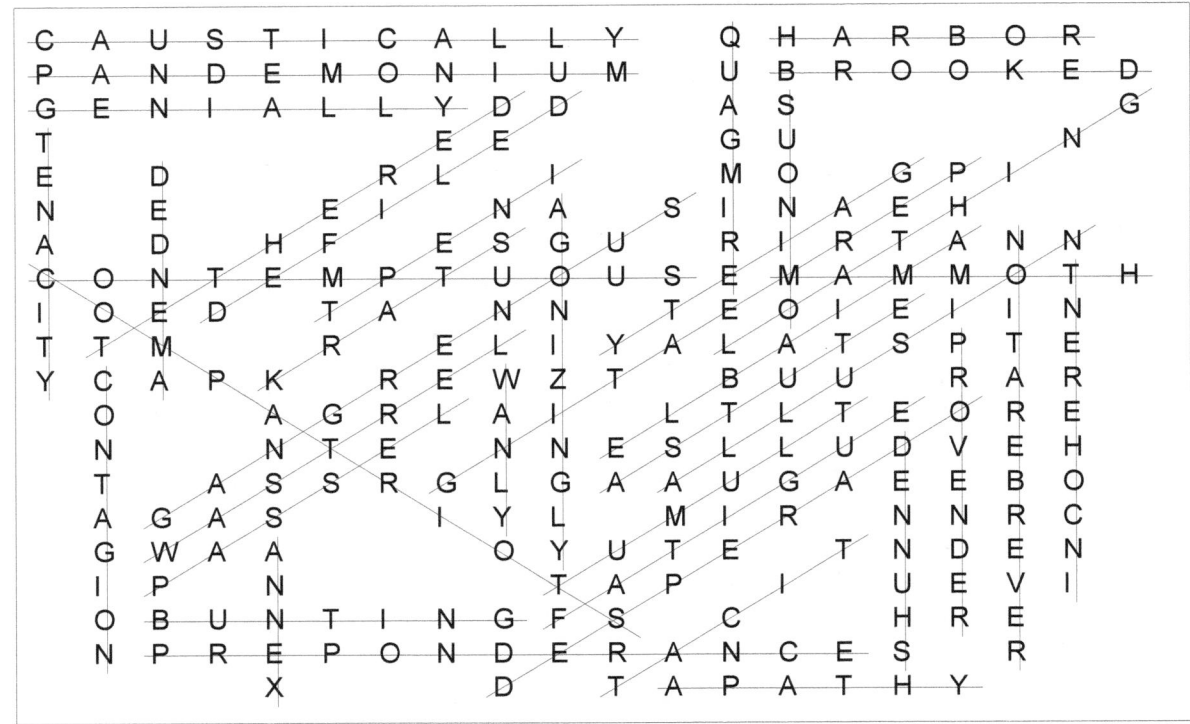

A bad influence; the spreading of an idea (9)
A bunch; many (6)
Agitation of the mind or emotions; a disturbance (6)
An addition or auxiliary building (5)
An echo-like effect (13)
Bare; harsh; desolate (5)
Being physically or emotionally tired (7)
Capable of burning; in a fiery manner (11)
Deliberately avoided (7)
Desperate outlaw (9)
Disjointed; not in an orderly manner (10)
Feeling of repulsion (8)
Festivity; happiness (6)
Fixed; corrected (7)
Food for animals (9)
Good-natured; friendly (7)
Having decaying bodily tissues (10)
Holding or sticking to something persistently (8)
Huge (7)
In a way showing one tired or sad (5)
Incompetent (5)
Indifference (6)
Indirect reference (8)
Kindly; pleasantly (8)
Majority (13)
One who wastes things (7)
Penetrating; spreading throughout (10)
People from one's own country or team (11)
Polluted (7)
Scornful (12)
Shrewd; smart concerning one's own affairs (6)
Soft, muddy land (8)
Strips of material in patriotic colors used for festive decorations (7)
Threatening (7)
Tied with a short rope or string (8)
To shelter (6)
Tolerated (7)
Unspoken (5)
Wild uproar (11)
With great pain or difficult (11)

Across Five Aprils Vocabulary Word Search 3

ADMONITIONS	DISSIPATED	PERMEATING
AGONIZINGLY	ENDURANCE	PREOCCUPATION
ALLUSION	FATIGUE	PROVENDER
AMENDED	GAIETY	QUAGMIRE
AMIABLE	GANGRENOUS	REITERATED
ANNEX	GENIALLY	REVERBERATION
APATHY	HARBOR	SHUNNED
ASTUTE	IMMINENCE	STARK
BROOKED	INCOHERENT	TACIT
BUNTING	INEPT	TENACITY
COMPATRIOTS	IRONCLADS	TETHERED
CONTAGION	LOATHING	TUMULT
CREDENCE	MAMMOTH	TYRANNICAL
CULPRITS	OMINOUS	VINDICTIVENESS
DEFILED	PANDEMONIUM	WANLY
DESPERADO	PASSEL	WASTREL

Across Five Aprils Vocabulary Word Search 3 Answer Key

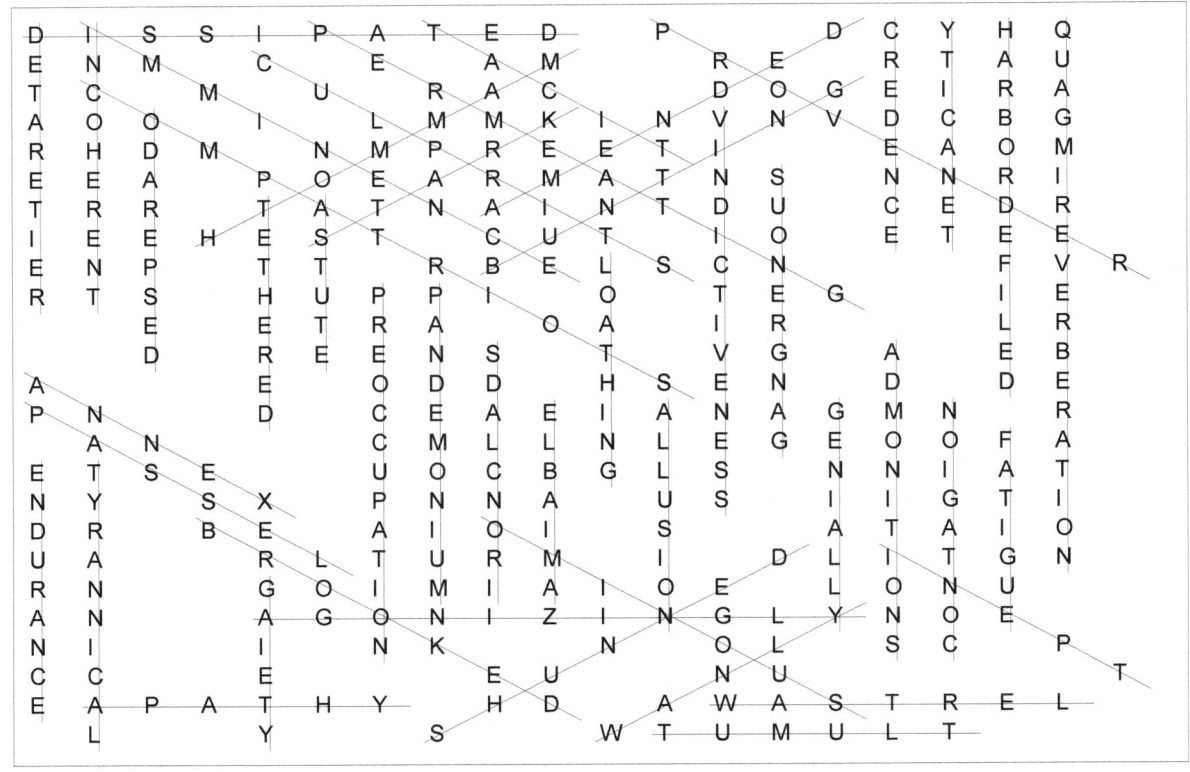

ADMONITIONS	DISSIPATED	PERMEATING
AGONIZINGLY	ENDURANCE	PREOCCUPATION
ALLUSION	FATIGUE	PROVENDER
AMENDED	GAIETY	QUAGMIRE
AMIABLE	GANGRENOUS	REITERATED
ANNEX	GENIALLY	REVERBERATION
APATHY	HARBOR	SHUNNED
ASTUTE	IMMINENCE	STARK
BROOKED	INCOHERENT	TACIT
BUNTING	INEPT	TENACITY
COMPATRIOTS	IRONCLADS	TETHERED
CONTAGION	LOATHING	TUMULT
CREDENCE	MAMMOTH	TYRANNICAL
CULPRITS	OMINOUS	VINDICTIVENESS
DEFILED	PANDEMONIUM	WANLY
DESPERADO	PASSEL	WASTREL

Across Five Aprils Vocabulary Word Search 4

```
G E N I A L L Y H G P M O M I N O U S M
Q T B J X L R W G N T A A M D W N S S G D
B T R H Z Y H I V Y N M J E G Q T T T E K
L X E V C Z T P H J D M K D X T L S X W
T F I M J A Y T N P E O F N P T P T E J
H R T V E T A J C C M T K E C E Z S N B
C A E M S P S Y F O O H N M R K P N N P
U D R B A T Y R A N N I C A L E S S A P
L E A B U M A L K O I T D O S J B U H D
P N T C O N E R I H U O A C Y T J O R Y
R N E L R R T S K S M T E G T B U U E J
I U D Q T E U I C X H W N V I R X T V D
T H S S T L D W N I X A D I C O T P E Q
S S A L L Y T E N G E N U N A O N M R S
A W A A P T H G N K C L R D N K D E B C
G T N M I E P S Z C N Y A I E E I T E X
O M P C I I S N B P E L N C T D S N R C
N R A L N A B X J R N S C T V E S O A G
I T W B F G B T S O I K E I X F I C T B
Z C G J K L C L M V M F T V G I P B I S
I F A T I G U E E E M S U E P L A J O N
N S B Z G H Q G Z N I T M N X E T T N K
G Q U A G M I R E D S S U E Y D E B Y D
L J I N C O H E R E N T L S K R D G K T
Y T E T H E R E D R L S T S P S M M T X
```

AGONIZINGLY	DISSIPATED	PROVENDER
ALLUSION	ENDURANCE	QUAGMIRE
AMENDED	FATIGUE	REITERATED
AMIABLE	GAIETY	REVERBERATION
ANNEX	GENIALLY	SHUNNED
APATHY	HARBOR	STARK
ASTUTE	IMMINENCE	TACIT
BROOKED	INCOHERENT	TENACITY
BUNTING	INEPT	TETHERED
CONTAGION	LOATHING	TUMULT
CONTEMPTUOUS	MAMMOTH	TYRANNICAL
CREDENCE	OMINOUS	VINDICTIVENESS
CULPRITS	PANDEMONIUM	WANLY
DEFILED	PASSEL	WASTREL
DESPERADO	PERMEATING	

Across Five Aprils Vocabulary Word Search 4 Answer Key

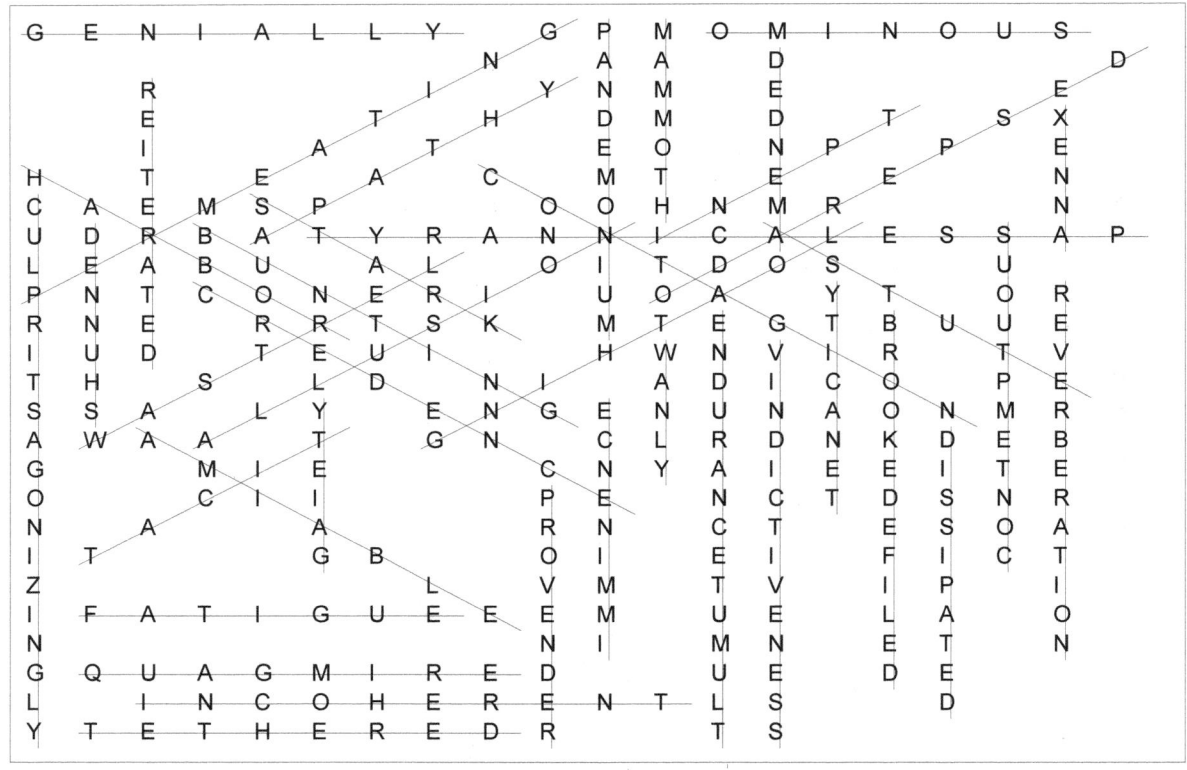

AGONIZINGLY	DISSIPATED	PROVENDER
ALLUSION	ENDURANCE	QUAGMIRE
AMENDED	FATIGUE	REITERATED
AMIABLE	GAIETY	REVERBERATION
ANNEX	GENIALLY	SHUNNED
APATHY	HARBOR	STARK
ASTUTE	IMMINENCE	TACIT
BROOKED	INCOHERENT	TENACITY
BUNTING	INEPT	TETHERED
CONTAGION	LOATHING	TUMULT
CONTEMPTUOUS	MAMMOTH	TYRANNICAL
CREDENCE	OMINOUS	VINDICTIVENESS
CULPRITS	PANDEMONIUM	WANLY
DEFILED	PASSEL	WASTREL
DESPERADO	PERMEATING	

Across Five Aprils Vocabulary Crossword 1

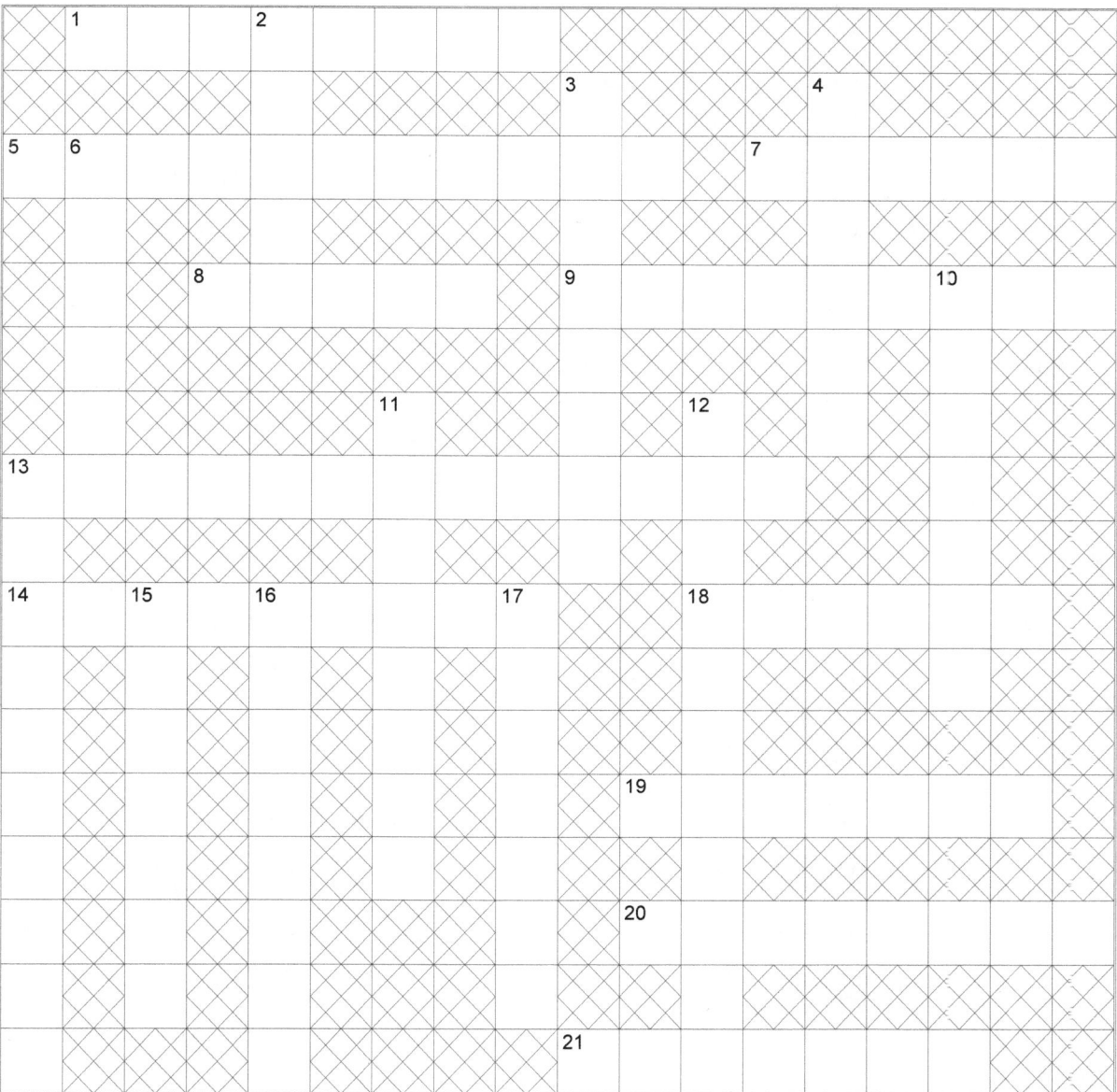

Across
1. Kindly; pleasantly
5. Wild uproar
7. To shelter
8. Bare; harsh; desolate
9. Food for animals
13. An echo-like effect
14. 19th century war ships having sides with metal plates as armor
18. A bunch; many
19. Tolerated
20. Feeling of repulsion
21. One who wastes things

Down
2. Incompetent
3. People charged with crimes
4. Festivity; happiness
6. Shrewd; smart concerning one's own affairs
10. Polluted
11. Holding or sticking to something persistently
12. People from one's own country or team
13. Said or did something repeatedly
15. Threatening
16. Believability
17. Deliberately avoided

Across Five Aprils Vocabulary Crossword 1 Answer Key

	1 G	E	N	2 I	A	L	L	Y				
				N					3 C		4 G	
5 P	6 A	N	D	E	M	O	N	I	U	M	7 H	A	R	B	O	R
	S			P					L		I	
	T		8 S	T	A	R	K		9 P	R	O	V	E	N	10 D	E	R
	U								R		T		E
	T				11 T			12 C		Y		F
13 R	E	V	E	R	B	E	R	A	T	I	O	N		I
E					N			S		M			L
14 I	15 R	O	16 N	C	L	A	17 D	S		18 P	A	S	S	E	L
T	M		R				C			H			U			A			D
E	I		E				I			U			
R	N		D				T		19 B	R	O	O	K	E	D
A	O		E				Y			N			I
T	U		N						20 L	O	A	T	H	I	N	G
E	S		C						E				T
D			E				21 W	A	S	T	R	E	L

Across
1. Kindly; pleasantly
5. Wild uproar
7. To shelter
8. Bare; harsh; desolate
9. Food for animals
13. An echo-like effect
14. 19th century war ships having sides with metal plates as armor
18. A bunch; many
19. Tolerated
20. Feeling of repulsion
21. One who wastes things

Down
2. Incompetent
3. People charged with crimes
4. Festivity; happiness
6. Shrewd; smart concerning one's own affairs
10. Polluted
11. Holding or sticking to something persistently
12. People from one's own country or team
13. Said or did something repeatedly
15. Threatening
16. Believability
17. Deliberately avoided

Across Five Aprils Vocabulary Crossword 2

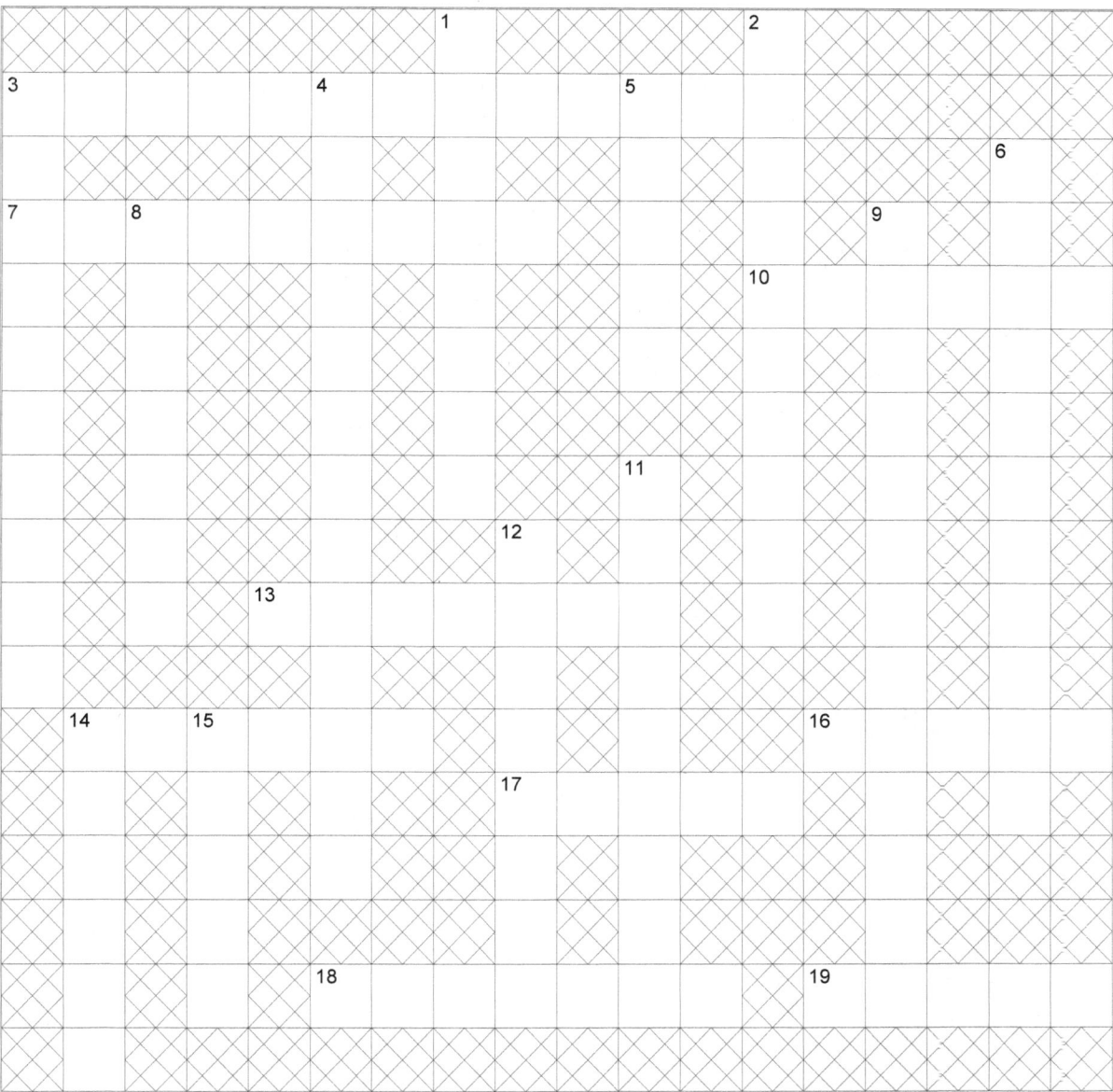

Across
3. An echo-like effect
7. 19th century war ships having sides with metal plates as armor
10. To shelter
13. Polluted
14. Shrewd; smart concerning one's own affairs
16. In a way showing one tired or sad
17. Bare; harsh; desolate
18. Fixed; corrected
19. An addition or auxiliary building

Down
1. Believability
2. Disjointed; not in an orderly manner
3. Said or did something repeatedly
4. Defiantly; in a hostile manner
5. Incompetent
6. With great pain or difficult
8. Threatening
9. Something that engrosses the mind
11. Strength over a long period of time
12. Indirect reference
14. Indifference
15. Unspoken

Across Five Aprils Vocabulary Crossword 2 Answer Key

						¹C			²I			
³R	E	V	⁴E	R	B	E	R	⁵A	T	I	O	N
E			E			E		N		C		⁶A
⁷I	⁸R	O	N	C	L	A	D	S		O	⁹P	G
T	M		L			E		P		¹⁰H	A	R	B	O	R
E	I		I			N		T		E		E			N
R	N		G			C				R		O			I
A	O		E			E		¹¹E		E		C			Z
T	U		R		¹²A			N		N		C			I
E	S		¹³D	E	F	I	L	E	D		T		U			N
D			N			L		U			P		G
	¹⁴A	¹⁵S	T	U	T	E		U		R		¹⁶W	A	N	L	Y
		P	A	L			¹⁷S	T	A	R	K		T		Y
		A	C	Y			I		N			I
		T	I				O		C			O
		H	¹⁸T	A	M	E	N	D	E	D		¹⁹A	N	N	E	X
		Y										

Across
3. An echo-like effect
7. 19th century war ships having sides with metal plates as armor
10. To shelter
13. Polluted
14. Shrewd; smart concerning one's own affairs
16. In a way showing one tired or sad
17. Bare; harsh; desolate
18. Fixed; corrected
19. An addition or auxiliary building

Down
1. Believability
2. Disjointed; not in an orderly manner
3. Said or did something repeatedly
4. Defiantly; in a hostile manner
5. Incompetent
6. With great pain or difficult
8. Threatening
9. Something that engrosses the mind
11. Strength over a long period of time
12. Indirect reference
14. Indifference
15. Unspoken

Across Five Aprils Vocabulary Crossword 3

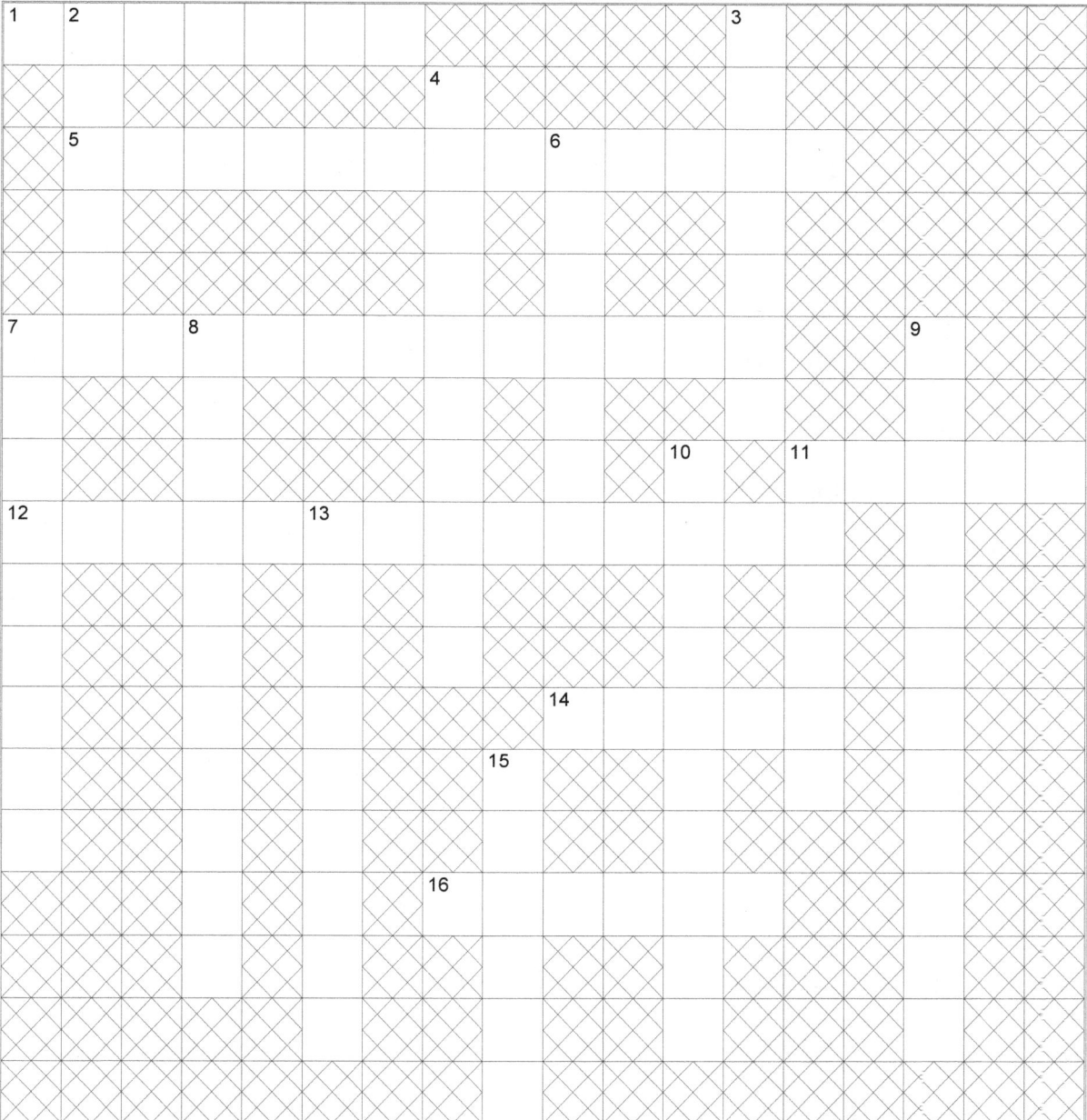

Across
1. Deliberately avoided
5. An echo-like effect
7. Majority
11. An addition or auxiliary building
12. Revengefulness
14. Incompetent
16. Festivity; happiness

Down
2. To shelter
3. Tolerated
4. Penetrating; spreading throughout
6. Good-natured; friendly
7. Food for animals
8. Wild uproar
9. Scornful
10. Said or did something repeatedly
11. Shrewd; smart concerning one's own affairs
13. A bad influence; the spreading of an idea
15. Indifference

Across Five Aprils Vocabulary Crossword 3 Answer Key

Across
1. Deliberately avoided
5. An echo-like effect
7. Majority
11. An addition or auxiliary building
12. Revengefulness
14. Incompetent
16. Festivity; happiness

Down
2. To shelter
3. Tolerated
4. Penetrating; spreading throughout
6. Good-natured; friendly
7. Food for animals
8. Wild uproar
9. Scornful
10. Said or did something repeatedly
11. Shrewd; smart concerning one's own affairs
13. A bad influence; the spreading of an idea
15. Indifference

Across Five Aprils Vocabulary Crossword 4

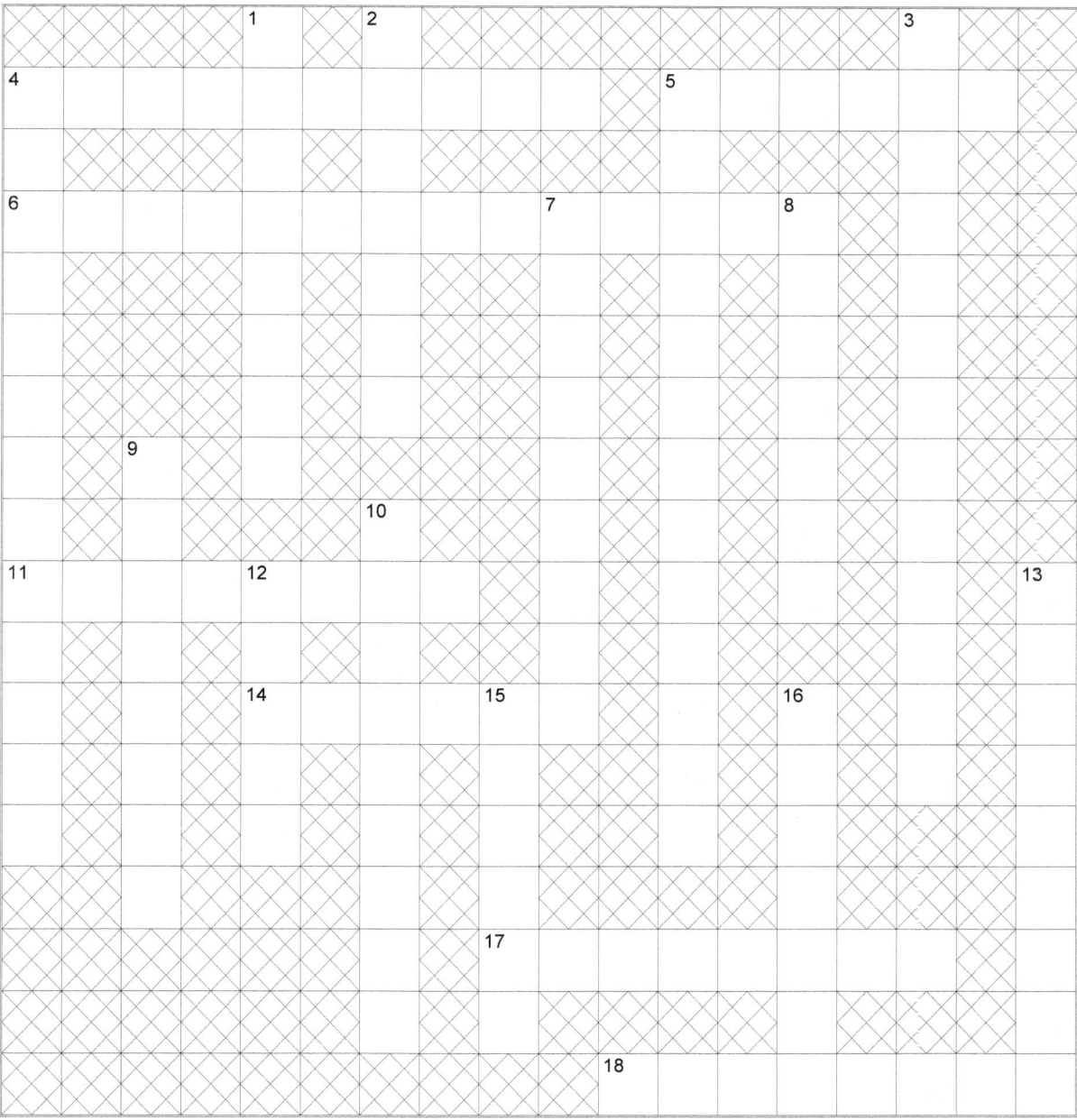

Across
4. Said or did something repeatedly
5. A bunch; many
6. Revengefulness
11. Indirect reference
14. Shrewd; smart concerning one's own affairs
17. Feeling of repulsion
18. Soft, muddy land

Down
1. Kindly; pleasantly
2. One who wastes things
3. Defiantly; in a hostile manner
4. An echo-like effect
5. Majority
7. Strength over a long period of time
8. Deliberately avoided
9. People charged with crimes
10. A bad influence; the spreading of an idea
12. Bare; harsh; desolate
13. The quality of being about to happen
15. Agitation of the mind or emotions; a disturbance
16. Strips of material in patriotic colors used for festive decorations

Across Five Aprils Vocabulary Crossword 4 Answer Key

			¹G		²W							³B	
⁴R	E	I	T	E	R	A	T	E	D		⁵P	A	S	S	E	L
E			N		S						R				L	
⁶V	I	N	D	I	C	T	⁷I	V	E	N	⁸E	S	S		L	
E			A		R		N				P		H		I	
R			L		E		D				O		U		G	
B			L		L		U				N		N		E	
E		⁹C	Y				R				D		N		R	
R		U		¹⁰C			A				E		E		E	
¹¹A	L	L	¹²S	I	O	N		N			R		D		N	¹³I
T		P		T		N		C			A				T	M
I		R	¹⁴A	S	T	¹⁵U	T	E			N	¹⁶B			L	M
O		I	R		A		U				C		U			Y	I
N		T	K		G		M				E		N				N
		S			I		U						T				E
					¹⁷O		L	O	A	T	H	I	N	G			N
					N		T						N				C
								¹⁸Q	U	A	G	M	I	R	E	

Across
4. Said or did something repeatedly
5. A bunch; many
6. Revengefulness
11. Indirect reference
14. Shrewd; smart concerning one's own affairs
17. Feeling of repulsion
18. Soft, muddy land

Down
1. Kindly; pleasantly
2. One who wastes things
3. Defiantly; in a hostile manner
4. An echo-like effect
5. Majority
7. Strength over a long period of time
8. Deliberately avoided
9. People charged with crimes
10. A bad influence; the spreading of an idea
12. Bare; harsh; desolate
13. The quality of being about to happen
15. Agitation of the mind or emotions; a disturbance
16. Strips of material in patriotic colors used for festive decorations

Across Five Aprils Vocabulary Juggle Letters 1

1. OTISSLABITINO = 1. _____
   People who wanted no more slavery

2. SWARLET = 2. _____
   One who wastes things

3. EERSODPDA = 3. _____
   Desperate outlaw

4. NIMSOOU = 4. _____
   Threatening

5. LEEDFDI = 5. _____
   Polluted

6. EAGPTRMINE = 6. _____
   Penetrating; spreading throughout

7. ENOPTOTMSUCU = 7. _____
   Scornful

8. YALGENIL = 8. _____
   Kindly; pleasantly

9. MOMTHAM = 9. _____
   Huge

10. YITEGA = 10. _____
    Festivity; happiness

11. NHNDUSE = 11. _____
    Deliberately avoided

12. IONGNAOTC = 12. _____
    A bad influence; the spreading of an idea

13. EENROVRDP = 13. _____
    Food for animals

14. AEXNN = 14. _____
    An addition or auxiliary building

15. CCERNDEE = 15. _____
    Believability

Across Five Aprils Vocabulary Juggle Letters 1 Answer Key

1. OTISSLABITINO = 1. ABOLITIONISTS
   People who wanted no more slavery

2. SWARLET = 2. WASTREL
   One who wastes things

3. EERSODPDA = 3. DESPERADO
   Desperate outlaw

4. NIMSOOU = 4. OMINOUS
   Threatening

5. LEEDFDI = 5. DEFILED
   Polluted

6. EAGPTRMINE = 6. PERMEATING
   Penetrating; spreading throughout

7. ENOPTOTMSUCU = 7. CONTEMPTUOUS
   Scornful

8. YALGENIL = 8. GENIALLY
   Kindly; pleasantly

9. MOMTHAM = 9. MAMMOTH
   Huge

10. YITEGA = 10. GAIETY
    Festivity; happiness

11. NHNDUSE = 11. SHUNNED
    Deliberately avoided

12. IONGNAOTC = 12. CONTAGION
    A bad influence; the spreading of an idea

13. EENROVRDP = 13. PROVENDER
    Food for animals

14. AEXNN = 14. ANNEX
    An addition or auxiliary building

15. CCERNDEE = 15. CREDENCE
    Believability

Across Five Aprils Vocabulary Juggle Letters 2

1. DMANEED = 1. _____
   Fixed; corrected

2. TLRESWA = 2. _____
   One who wastes things

3. OTESUMCUPOTN = 3. _____
   Scornful

4. SICRDAOLN = 4. _____
   19th century war ships having sides with metal plates as armor

5. OBRHAR = 5. _____
   To shelter

6. RKTSA = 6. _____
   Bare; harsh; desolate

7. YACITTEN = 7. _____
   Holding or sticking to something persistently

8. OTLHNAIG = 8. _____
   Feeling of repulsion

9. SAPLSE = 9. _____
   A bunch; many

10. MABALEI = 10. _____
    Good-natured; friendly

11. DRAEOSEDP = 11. _____
    Desperate outlaw

12. NANXE = 12. _____
    An addition or auxiliary building

13. MOSAOTNNIID = 13. _____
    Reprimands

14. IBAILSONSIOTT = 14. _____
    People who wanted no more slavery

15. UULTTM = 15. _____
    Agitation of the mind or emotions; a disturbance

Across Five Aprils Vocabulary Juggle Letters 2 Answer Key

1. DMANEED = 1. AMENDED
Fixed; corrected

2. TLRESWA = 2. WASTREL
One who wastes things

3. OTESUMCUPOTN = 3. CONTEMPTUOUS
Scornful

4. SICRDAOLN = 4. IRONCLADS
19th century war ships having sides with metal plates as armor

5. OBRHAR = 5. HARBOR
To shelter

6. RKTSA = 6. STARK
Bare; harsh; desolate

7. YACITTEN = 7. TENACITY
Holding or sticking to something persistently

8. OTLHNAIG = 8. LOATHING
Feeling of repulsion

9. SAPLSE = 9. PASSEL
A bunch; many

10. MABALEI = 10. AMIABLE
Good-natured; friendly

11. DRAEOSEDP = 11. DESPERADO
Desperate outlaw

12. NANXE = 12. ANNEX
An addition or auxiliary building

13. MOSAOTNNIID = 13. ADMONITIONS
Reprimands

14. IBAILSONSIOTT = 14. ABOLITIONISTS
People who wanted no more slavery

15. UULTTM = 15. TUMULT
Agitation of the mind or emotions; a disturbance

Across Five Aprils Vocabulary Juggle Letters 3

1. NAEUDONMMPI = 1. _____
   Wild uproar

2. EENDCCRE = 2. _____
   Believability

3. YCCIUASTLAL = 3. _____
   Capable of burning; in a fiery manner

4. TUATES = 4. _____
   Shrewd; smart concerning one's own affairs

5. CINETYTA = 5. _____
   Holding or sticking to something persistent y

6. LGINYAEL = 6. _____
   Kindly; pleasantly

7. RDETEHTE = 7. _____
   Tied with a short rope or string

8. PDRVOENER = 8. _____
   Food for animals

9. YIANTLNARC = 9. _____
   Oppressively domineering

10. INAGZGNYLOI = 10. _____
    With great pain or difficult

11. NYALW = 11. _____
    In a way showing one tired or sad

12. OIUSMON = 12. _____
    Threatening

13. EPPREARONNCDE = 13. _____
    Majority

14. ELSPAS = 14. _____
    A bunch; many

15. DEFDIEL = 15. _____
    Polluted

Across Five Aprils Vocabulary Juggle Letters 3 Answer Key

1. NAEUDONMMPI = 1. PANDEMONIUM
Wild uproar

2. EENDCCRE = 2. CREDENCE
Believability

3. YCCIUASTLAL = 3. CAUSTICALLY
Capable of burning; in a fiery manner

4. TUATES = 4. ASTUTE
Shrewd; smart concerning one's own affairs

5. CINETYTA = 5. TENACITY
Holding or sticking to something persistently

6. LGINYAEL = 6. GENIALLY
Kindly; pleasantly

7. RDETEHTE = 7. TETHERED
Tied with a short rope or string

8. PDRVOENER = 8. PROVENDER
Food for animals

9. YIANTLNARC = 9. TYRANNICAL
Oppressively domineering

10. INAGZGNYLOI =10. AGONIZINGLY
With great pain or difficult

11. NYALW =11. WANLY
In a way showing one tired or sad

12. OIUSMON =12. OMINOUS
Threatening

13. EPPREARONNCDE =13. PREPONDERANCE
Majority

14. ELSPAS =14. PASSEL
A bunch; many

15. DEFDIEL =15. DEFILED
Polluted

Across Five Aprils Vocabulary Juggle Letters 4

1. IACTT = 1. _____
   Unspoken

2. ETUAST = 2. _____
   Shrewd; smart concerning one's own affairs

3. NEIPT = 3. _____
   Incompetent

4. DEAEMDN = 4. _____
   Fixed; corrected

5. LSSAPE = 5. _____
   A bunch; many

6. KRTSA = 6. _____
   Bare; harsh; desolate

7. TULTUM = 7. _____
   Agitation of the mind or emotions; a disturbance

8. LSRITCPU = 8. _____
   People charged with crimes

9. NGLYIAEL = 9. _____
   Kindly; pleasantly

10. MEICNNEMI =10. _____
    The quality of being about to happen

11. ESLRAWT =11. _____
    One who wastes things

12. ROODBKE =12. _____
    Tolerated

13. INVVEESSTINDCI =13. _____
    Revengefulness

14. SBOILTTNOIISA =14. _____
    People who wanted no more slavery

15. MUNOPCTETOSU =15. _____
    Scornful

Across Five Aprils Vocabulary Juggle Letters 4 Answer Key

1. IACTT = 1. TACIT
Unspoken

2. ETUAST = 2. ASTUTE
Shrewd; smart concerning one's own affairs

3. NEIPT = 3. INEPT
Incompetent

4. DEAEMDN = 4. AMENDED
Fixed; corrected

5. LSSAPE = 5. PASSEL
A bunch; many

6. KRTSA = 6. STARK
Bare; harsh; desolate

7. TULTUM = 7. TUMULT
Agitation of the mind or emotions; a disturbance

8. LSRITCPU = 8. CULPRITS
People charged with crimes

9. NGLYIAEL = 9. GENIALLY
Kindly; pleasantly

10. MEICNNEMI = 10. IMMINENCE
The quality of being about to happen

11. ESLRAWT = 11. WASTREL
One who wastes things

12. ROODBKE = 12. BROOKED
Tolerated

13. INVVEESSTINDCI = 13. VINDICTIVENESS
Revengefulness

14. SBOILTTNOIISA = 14. ABOLITIONISTS
People who wanted no more slavery

15. MUNOPCTETOSU = 15. CONTEMPTUOUS
Scornful

ABOLITIONISTS	People who wanted no more slavery
ADMONITIONS	Reprimands
AGONIZINGLY	With great pain or difficult
ALLUSION	Indirect reference
AMENDED	Fixed; corrected
AMIABLE	Good-natured; friendly

ANNEX	An addition or auxiliary building
APATHY	Indifference
ASTUTE	Shrewd; smart concerning one's own affairs
BELLIGERENTLY	Defiantly; in a hostile manner
BROOKED	Tolerated
BUNTING	Strips of material in patriotic colors used for festive decorations

CAUSTICALLY	Capable of burning; in a fiery manner
COMPATRIOTS	People from one's own country or team
CONTAGION	A bad influence; the spreading of an idea
CONTEMPTUOUS	Scornful
CREDENCE	Believability
CULPRITS	People charged with crimes

DEFILED	Polluted
DESPERADO	Desperate outlaw
DISSIPATED	Dispersed; sent or went away
ENDURANCE	Strength over a long period of time
FATIGUE	Being physically or emotionally tired
GAIETY	Festivity; happiness

GANGRENOUS	Having decaying bodily tissues
GENIALLY	Kindly; pleasantly
HARBOR	To shelter
IMMINENCE	The quality of being about to happen
INCOHERENT	Disjointed; not in an orderly manner
INEPT	Incompetent

IRONCLADS	19th century war ships having sides with metal plates as armor
LOATHING	Feeling of repulsion
MAMMOTH	Huge
OMINOUS	Threatening
PANDEMONIUM	Wild uproar
PASSEL	A bunch; many

PERMEATING	Penetrating; spreading throughout
PREOCCUPATION	Something that engrosses the mind
PREPONDERANCE	Majority
PROVENDER	Food for animals
QUAGMIRE	Soft, muddy land
REITERATED	Said or did something repeatedly

REVERBERATION	An echo-like effect
SHUNNED	Deliberately avoided
STARK	Bare; harsh; desolate
TACIT	Unspoken
TENACITY	Holding or sticking to something persistently
TETHERED	Tied with a short rope or string

TUMULT	Agitation of the mind or emotions; a disturbance
TYRANNICAL	Oppressively domineering
VINDICTIVENESS	Revengefulness
WANLY	In a way showing one tired or sad
WASTREL	One who wastes things

Across Five Aprils Vocabulary

GANGRENOUS	AMENDED	MAMMOTH	QUAGMIRE	CONTAGION
ANNEX	INCOHERENT	APATHY	ABOLITIONISTS	GAIETY
CREDENCE	CULPRITS	FREE SPACE	TENACITY	WANLY
PREOCCUPATION	BUNTING	PERMEATING	PASSEL	WASTREL
DISSIPATED	GENIALLY	OMINOUS	INEPT	TACIT

Across Five Aprils Vocabulary

STARK	IMMINENCE	ADMONITIONS	AGONIZINGLY	COMPATRIOTS
CONTEMPTUOUS	ALLUSION	DEFILED	LOATHING	DESPERADO
BROOKED	TYRANNICAL	FREE SPACE	REITERATED	TETHERED
VINDICTIVENESS	CAUSTICALLY	PROVENDER	AMIABLE	REVERBERATION
ASTUTE	ENDURANCE	PREPONDERANCE	FATIGUE	HARBOR

Across Five Aprils Vocabulary

TUMULT	TENACITY	TYRANNICAL	CONTAGION	BELLIGERENTLY
REVERBERATION	ANNEX	SHUNNED	GENIALLY	PANDEMONIUM
PROVENDER	PREPONDERANCE	FREE SPACE	DESPERADO	PASSEL
INEPT	VINDICTIVENESS	AMIABLE	PREOCCUPATION	LOATHING
CONTEMPTUOUS	BUNTING	BROOKED	TETHERED	DISSIPATED

Across Five Aprils Vocabulary

IRONCLADS	CAUSTICALLY	OMINOUS	COMPATRIOTS	WANLY
GAIETY	APATHY	HARBOR	ALLUSION	GANGRENOUS
CREDENCE	AMENDED	FREE SPACE	FATIGUE	QUAGMIRE
IMMINENCE	REITERATED	WASTREL	MAMMOTH	INCOHERENT
PERMEATING	DEFILED	ASTUTE	STARK	AGONIZINGLY

Across Five Aprils Vocabulary

GAIETY	PREPONDERANCE	SHUNNED	AGONIZINGLY	MAMMOTH
GENIALLY	TYRANNICAL	TENACITY	CULPRITS	REITERATED
OMINOUS	QUAGMIRE	FREE SPACE	INEPT	TETHERED
AMIABLE	TACIT	REVERBERATION	DEFILED	ABOLITIONISTS
STARK	GANGRENOUS	WANLY	CONTAGION	DISSIPATED

Across Five Aprils Vocabulary

BELLIGERENTLY	PANDEMONIUM	CONTEMPTUOUS	ENDURANCE	HARBOR
VINDICTIVENESS	CAUSTICALLY	AMENDED	PERMEATING	INCOHERENT
ASTUTE	PASSEL	FREE SPACE	ANNEX	PROVENDER
BUNTING	FATIGUE	TUMULT	COMPATRIOTS	CREDENCE
ALLUSION	IRONCLADS	IMMINENCE	BROOKED	WASTREL

Across Five Aprils Vocabulary

CAUSTICALLY	TYRANNICAL	BUNTING	BROOKED	MAMMOTH
APATHY	CONTAGION	ABOLITIONISTS	PERMEATING	AMENDED
PROVENDER	WANLY	FREE SPACE	CONTEMPTUOUS	COMPATRIOTS
SHUNNED	DESPERADO	PASSEL	GANGRENOUS	QUAGMIRE
ADMONITIONS	ENDURANCE	IRONCLADS	PREPONDERANCE	CULPRITS

Across Five Aprils Vocabulary

DEFILED	CREDENCE	INCOHERENT	DISSIPATED	PANDEMONIUM
IMMINENCE	ALLUSION	TETHERED	AMIABLE	STARK
TACIT	REITERATED	FREE SPACE	REVERBERATION	VINDICTIVENESS
BELLIGERENTLY	WASTREL	OMINOUS	ANNEX	ASTUTE
HARBOR	FATIGUE	INEPT	PREOCCUPATION	AGONIZINGLY

Across Five Aprils Vocabulary

SHUNNED	PROVENDER	PASSEL	GAIETY	WANLY
REITERATED	FATIGUE	CULPRITS	INCOHERENT	ALLUSION
TETHERED	DISSIPATED	FREE SPACE	CREDENCE	ASTUTE
ABOLITIONISTS	TYRANNICAL	PREOCCUPATION	LOATHING	PERMEATING
GANGRENOUS	AMIABLE	HARBOR	REVERBERATION	ADMONITIONS

Across Five Aprils Vocabulary

CONTEMPTUOUS	CAUSTICALLY	ENDURANCE	VINDICTIVENESS	IMMINENCE
TUMULT	COMPATRIOTS	PANDEMONIUM	TENACITY	TACIT
BROOKED	DEFILED	FREE SPACE	ANNEX	APATHY
STARK	IRONCLADS	DESPERADO	WASTREL	QUAGMIRE
OMINOUS	BELLIGERENTLY	CONTAGION	BUNTING	INEPT

Across Five Aprils Vocabulary

ABOLITIONISTS	ENDURANCE	SHUNNED	PASSEL	PREOCCUPATION
GAIETY	PERMEATING	INEPT	GANGRENOUS	CREDENCE
DISSIPATED	AGONIZINGLY	FREE SPACE	AMENDED	LOATHING
DEFILED	QUAGMIRE	STARK	TUMULT	TETHERED
ADMONITIONS	BUNTING	HARBOR	DESPERADO	PROVENDER

Across Five Aprils Vocabulary

PANDEMONIUM	AMIABLE	CAUSTICALLY	ANNEX	VINDICTIVENESS
REITERATED	IRONCLADS	MAMMOTH	ALLUSION	WANLY
REVERBERATION	COMPATRIOTS	FREE SPACE	IMMINENCE	ASTUTE
PREPONDERANCE	CONTAGION	TYRANNICAL	BELLIGERENTLY	TENACITY
BROOKED	APATHY	FATIGUE	TACIT	OMINOUS

Across Five Aprils Vocabulary

REITERATED	PERMEATING	AGONIZINGLY	HARBOR	ASTUTE
PREOCCUPATION	BUNTING	VINDICTIVENESS	CAUSTICALLY	STARK
PASSEL	INEPT	FREE SPACE	FATIGUE	DESPERADO
CONTEMPTUOUS	APATHY	TYRANNICAL	ABOLITIONISTS	DEFILED
OMINOUS	INCOHERENT	TUMULT	PROVENDER	PANDEMONIUM

Across Five Aprils Vocabulary

ENDURANCE	LOATHING	TETHERED	TACIT	IMMINENCE
IRONCLADS	GENIALLY	WASTREL	SHUNNED	MAMMOTH
AMENDED	QUAGMIRE	FREE SPACE	COMPATRIOTS	CONTAGION
BELLIGERENTLY	PREPONDERANCE	BROOKED	CULPRITS	REVERBERATION
DISSIPATED	GANGRENOUS	CREDENCE	AMIABLE	TENACITY

Across Five Aprils Vocabulary

PREPONDERANCE	WASTREL	ANNEX	INCOHERENT	PREOCCUPATION
ASTUTE	QUAGMIRE	AGONIZINGLY	BROOKED	AMENDED
PASSEL	TUMULT	FREE SPACE	FATIGUE	GANGRENOUS
GENIALLY	CONTAGION	REVERBERATION	PERMEATING	OMINOUS
SHUNNED	ENDURANCE	CAUSTICALLY	INEPT	CREDENCE

Across Five Aprils Vocabulary

TACIT	COMPATRIOTS	GAIETY	IRONCLADS	BUNTING
TETHERED	ADMONITIONS	MAMMOTH	REITERATED	IMMINENCE
VINDICTIVENESS	CONTEMPTUOUS	FREE SPACE	PROVENDER	STARK
DESPERADO	WANLY	LOATHING	ABOLITIONISTS	PANDEMONIUM
TYRANNICAL	CULPRITS	ALLUSION	DEFILED	HARBOR

Across Five Aprils Vocabulary

IMMINENCE	CAUSTICALLY	GENIALLY	WASTREL	ANNEX
VINDICTIVENESS	WANLY	ALLUSION	CULPRITS	PREOCCUPATION
SHUNNED	BUNTING	FREE SPACE	AGONIZINGLY	AMENDED
PROVENDER	AMIABLE	DESPERADO	TACIT	HARBOR
ASTUTE	PASSEL	PANDEMONIUM	TENACITY	APATHY

Across Five Aprils Vocabulary

GANGRENOUS	CREDENCE	FATIGUE	OMINOUS	ADMONITIONS
TETHERED	PREPONDERANCE	STARK	LOATHING	INEPT
QUAGMIRE	TYRANNICAL	FREE SPACE	COMPATRIOTS	ENDURANCE
CONTEMPTUOUS	TUMULT	REITERATED	ABOLITIONISTS	REVERBERATION
CONTAGION	IRONCLADS	INCOHERENT	DEFILED	MAMMOTH

Across Five Aprils Vocabulary

TACIT	GENIALLY	DEFILED	DISSIPATED	IMMINENCE
WANLY	ENDURANCE	HARBOR	CAUSTICALLY	STARK
ABOLITIONISTS	FATIGUE	FREE SPACE	CONTAGION	BUNTING
CULPRITS	CONTEMPTUOUS	SHUNNED	BROOKED	PREPONDERANCE
CREDENCE	PREOCCUPATION	PROVENDER	APATHY	TUMULT

Across Five Aprils Vocabulary

PERMEATING	BELLIGERENTLY	ANNEX	TYRANNICAL	ADMONITIONS
INEPT	AMENDED	TETHERED	LOATHING	REITERATED
GANGRENOUS	QUAGMIRE	FREE SPACE	DESPERADO	AGONIZINGLY
PASSEL	TENACITY	OMINOUS	INCOHERENT	REVERBERATION
WASTREL	VINDICTIVENESS	MAMMOTH	PANDEMONIUM	AMIABLE

Across Five Aprils Vocabulary

IMMINENCE	TUMULT	ANNEX	PANDEMONIUM	AGONIZINGLY
PROVENDER	CREDENCE	TYRANNICAL	TENACITY	MAMMOTH
GENIALLY	STARK	FREE SPACE	BELLIGERENTLY	COMPATRIOTS
PREPONDERANCE	WANLY	REITERATED	PASSEL	IRONCLADS
SHUNNED	DISSIPATED	REVERBERATION	QUAGMIRE	TACIT

Across Five Aprils Vocabulary

HARBOR	GAIETY	TETHERED	INCOHERENT	LOATHING
CONTEMPTUOUS	CONTAGION	APATHY	PERMEATING	ADMONITIONS
PREOCCUPATION	OMINOUS	FREE SPACE	VINDICTIVENESS	BROOKED
ENDURANCE	CULPRITS	ASTUTE	DEFILED	ABOLITIONISTS
FATIGUE	WASTREL	ALLUSION	CAUSTICALLY	GANGRENOUS

Across Five Aprils Vocabulary

IMMINENCE	QUAGMIRE	ALLUSION	TUMULT	GENIALLY
PANDEMONIUM	PROVENDER	DESPERADO	CAUSTICALLY	GANGRENOUS
WASTREL	TYRANNICAL	FREE SPACE	MAMMOTH	ANNEX
INEPT	APATHY	CONTEMPTUOUS	INCOHERENT	PASSEL
FATIGUE	CONTAGION	REVERBERATION	REITERATED	DISSIPATED

Across Five Aprils Vocabulary

BUNTING	VINDICTIVENESS	CREDENCE	DEFILED	ABOLITIONISTS
OMINOUS	AMIABLE	TENACITY	PERMEATING	STARK
COMPATRIOTS	AMENDED	FREE SPACE	PREPONDERANCE	ENDURANCE
HARBOR	GAIETY	BELLIGERENTLY	BROOKED	IRONCLADS
ASTUTE	AGONIZINGLY	SHUNNED	TETHERED	LOATHING

Across Five Aprils Vocabulary

WASTREL	REVERBERATION	GANGRENOUS	TETHERED	ABOLITIONISTS
GENIALLY	INEPT	AMIABLE	DISSIPATED	ASTUTE
PERMEATING	LOATHING	FREE SPACE	PASSEL	STARK
WANLY	CONTEMPTUOUS	DEFILED	CAUSTICALLY	INCOHERENT
FATIGUE	APATHY	ADMONITIONS	CULPRITS	ALLUSION

Across Five Aprils Vocabulary

TACIT	ANNEX	TYRANNICAL	IMMINENCE	GAIETY
CONTAGION	TUMULT	PREOCCUPATION	TENACITY	REITERATED
PANDEMONIUM	ENDURANCE	FREE SPACE	BROOKED	AMENDED
CREDENCE	QUAGMIRE	HARBOR	DESPERADO	OMINOUS
PREPONDERANCE	SHUNNED	MAMMOTH	PROVENDER	AGONIZINGLY

Across Five Aprils Vocabulary

AMIABLE	CREDENCE	LOATHING	ALLUSION	INEPT
TUMULT	PROVENDER	OMINOUS	BUNTING	FERMEATING
PREOCCUPATION	DISSIPATED	FREE SPACE	REVERBERATION	ADMONITIONS
PREPONDERANCE	MAMMOTH	CONTAGION	APATHY	SHUNNED
REITERATED	PASSEL	GENIALLY	TETHERED	ENDURANCE

Across Five Aprils Vocabulary

DESPERADO	FATIGUE	ASTUTE	PANDEMONIUM	CAUSTICALLY
AGONIZINGLY	CULPRITS	IMMINENCE	INCOHERENT	TACIT
WANLY	HARBOR	FREE SPACE	ABOLITIONISTS	VINDICTIVENESS
TYRANNICAL	COMPATRIOTS	TENACITY	QUAGMIRE	IRONCLADS
CONTEMPTUOUS	WASTREL	GAIETY	AMENDED	STARK

Across Five Aprils Vocabulary

TACIT	STARK	TETHERED	BROOKED	DEFILED
COMPATRIOTS	BELLIGERENTLY	LOATHING	AMIABLE	ENDURANCE
OMINOUS	APATHY	FREE SPACE	ABOLITIONISTS	CONTAGION
ADMONITIONS	ALLUSION	QUAGMIRE	PASSEL	FATIGUE
CREDENCE	CULPRITS	REVERBERATION	DISSIPATED	TENACITY

Across Five Aprils Vocabulary

INCOHERENT	HARBOR	AMENDED	IRONCLADS	TYRANNICAL
CONTEMPTUOUS	MAMMOTH	SHUNNED	VINDICTIVENESS	GANGRENOUS
BUNTING	CAUSTICALLY	FREE SPACE	AGONIZINGLY	GENIALLY
ANNEX	PROVENDER	WANLY	REITERATED	IMMINENCE
PERMEATING	INEPT	PREOCCUPATION	WASTREL	DESPERADO

Across Five Aprils Vocabulary

HARBOR	PREPONDERANCE	TENACITY	INCOHERENT	STARK
BELLIGERENTLY	ALLUSION	ABOLITIONISTS	AGONIZINGLY	CONTEMPTUOUS
ASTUTE	CULPRITS	FREE SPACE	ENDURANCE	LOATHING
APATHY	TETHERED	REVERBERATION	DESPERADO	CONTAGION
REITERATED	WANLY	GANGRENOUS	AMIABLE	DISSIPATED

Across Five Aprils Vocabulary

IRONCLADS	AMENDED	GENIALLY	OMINOUS	ADMONITIONS
PERMEATING	TACIT	CAUSTICALLY	MAMMOTH	TUMULT
BROOKED	VINDICTIVENESS	FREE SPACE	QUAGMIRE	ANNEX
PROVENDER	BUNTING	CREDENCE	DEFILED	COMPATRIOTS
PREOCCUPATION	PANDEMONIUM	TYRANNICAL	GAIETY	INEPT

www.ingramcontent.com/pod-product-compliance
Lightning Source LLC
LaVergne TN
LVHW081538060526
838200LV00048B/2123